The

NERVOUS FLYER'S
HANDBOOK

Your Portable Flight Coach

Kate L. Fellows

First published by Dog Ear Publishing
4010 W. 86th Street, Ste H
Indianapolis, IN 46268
www.dogearpublishing.net

ISBN: 978-160844-299-7

This book is printed on acid-free paper.

Printed in the United States of America

For Nicholas & Juliet

TABLE OF CONTENTS

SECTION 3: THE PHASES OF FLIGHT

SECTION 4: DISTRACTIONS

SECTION 5: SPECIAL ISSUES

SECTION 6: POST-FLIGHT

REFERENCE

INTRODUCTION

You're in the Right Book

If you're anywhere on the scale from slightly nervous to outright petrified when it comes to flying, and you want a coach with practical ideas to help you, you're in the right book.

And if you're looking for advice from someone who can actually relate to your feelings — an alternative to pilots and psychologists telling you how to "cure" your fear of flying — you are even *more* in the right book.

I am not a psychologist or a pilot; instead, I used to be like you. I am a former nervous flyer who has learned from over 20 years of reluctant frequent flying how to manage my nervousness about flight. I have the "expert passenger" perspective – how to think about flight, how to prepare, and how to cope once in the air (and maybe even enjoy it a bit).

I am not connected to the flight industry. I have zero motivation to sell more plane tickets, and I am not going to tell you the typical spiel about how your nervousness about flight is a "phobia" based on your "control issues," and you'd be fine if you just "breathe deeply" or listen to some new-agey relaxation music.

And here's why I'm not going to tell you those things: Your nervous feelings about flight are *valid*. Human flight is an unnatural concept, really. For all of human existence except for a recent blip in time, the only creatures in our sky were those who were born with wings.

Yet because of all that, flight is also ***absolutely amazing***. And wondrous, and practical, and manageable, and can add great value to your life, whether it's by keeping connected with family and friends, progressing in your work, or taking your dream vacation.

I have taken well over five hundred of domestic and overseas flights, including a 2-year run of flying every week up and down the west coast. I used to think I would die every time I stepped on a plane, but I forced myself to do it.

At some point, I decided to be proactive and start writing notes for myself over time – jotting down various thoughts on flight, how to prepare, ideas, quotes, activities and more to cope and comfort myself while flying. Those notes helped me remember each time I flew, and now it's in the form of this book. They have helped me numerous times, in a way that taking a fear-of-flying (FOF) class, therapy, and books written by pilots and psychologists could not.

In being able to quickly reference my notes before and during flight, I became my own "flight coach."

I did once take a pilot-led FOF class once that explained how flight works, but it was nothing more than what I could find online for free. Although I would never discourage anyone from taking such a class, it was a stretch to have a pilot, who is clearly not afraid of flying, try to relate to how I felt.

The other issue I found was that when you are in the ***moment*** of nervousness, fear, or outright panic, *your* *brain does not remember or process* very well the things you learned in a class. If I felt scared, trying to recall how the plane operates in turbulence wasn't much help. I wanted immediate reassurance right in front of me, with common sense and techniques on how to stay as relaxed as possible.

What I have found with FOF resources by psychologists is that they tend to be generic and unrealistic; plus I think it's ridiculous that a fear of flying would even be referred to as a "phobia" (the terms are aerophobia and aviphobia). And when you're nervous in flight, you are not necessarily in the state of mind to do some of the usual recommended techniques — perhaps you feel embarrassed or reluctant to try deep breaths, for example, with your fellow passengers merely inches away. Or you are unable to listen to that that new-agey "subconscious relaxation" music when you need it most – take-off or landing — because it's not even allowed.

I Can Relate

Opinions aside, most of the fear-of-flying resources out there today from pilots and psychologists *are* well-intended, and as your flight coach I would always encourage you to seek any and all help for easing your nervousness about flight.

But I provide the practical, time-tested advice of someone who can truly ***relate to how you feel***. A pilot is not nervous about flying, and the psychologist has a different lens altogether.

What I have assembled for you are more realistic "ways to think about flight" and techniques to use before you go and while you're in the air. I also focus on how to minimize your anxiety through better preparation, list tried and true ideas for effective distractions, talk through special issues, and even provide a few pep talks.

The difference I try to make for you is to validate your feelings, and provide a more practical, spell-it-out perspective. In **your moment of greatest need**, your brain wants immediate reminders, words of comfort, logic and familiarity. I take the approach as if I were sitting in the seat next to you during your flight, coaching you along.

And you won't be made to feel as if you have a **problem** just because you're nervous about flying. You don't. Many people that are at least a little nervous about flying. You are the majority, not the minority.

Still, life is too short to not to take that flight – to not see family, friends, places of interest, or not pursue job opportunities just because flying freaks you out. It is all of those things that have kept me motivated to step on that plane many times, and from those experiences, I share my ideas with you.

When, Where & How To Use This Book

Use this book as your "portable flight coach." I designed it with that purpose – small and discreet, a comprehensive table of contents, no flashy or colorful photos or graphics, short segments that are easy to read and high-light, and blank pages in the back for your own notes. And unless you have opted for an electronic version, you don't even have to wait to pass through 10,000 feet to use it.

What you'll find in this book is a wide variety of *types* of advice. That's because as human beings, our moods and needs vary at any given minute. This book doesn't give you just one way to cope – it gives you many.

This book has 6 major sections:

- **Section 1: Ways to Think About Flight** – Use these chapters at any time to help frame your thinking about flight and keep things in perspective.
- **Section 2: Preparing to Fly** – Empower yourself and minimize anxiety triggers before your flight by preparing for flight in a variety of ways, including what to bring, what to wear, getting through vari-ous airport processes, and dealing with delays.
- **Section 3: Phases of Flight** – Provides coaching on what to expect and how to think about each major part of the flight from take-off, cruising, descent, and landing.
- **Section 4: Distractions** – Suggests a range of activ-ities to help keep your brain busy during flight.
- **Section 5: Special Issues** – Offers perspectives and coping techniques for a variety of situations you may or may not have control over during flight.
- **Section 6: Post-Flight:** Review what worked best for you, and help yourself even more next time, whether it's a return flight or next year's vacation.

I hope you can discover the same sense of peace that I have come to find when I fly. It might take some practice, but I am proof that it is possible.

Sincerely,
Kate Fellows

SECTION 1: WAYS TO THINK ABOUT FLIGHT

Chapter 1: You Are Not Alone

Just how many people are nervous about flying? An often-quoted number in various articles on the internet indicate 25 million people[1] in the US alone.

In addition, I did a survey of family, friends, and colleagues. This was a diverse mix consisting of 100 frequent and infrequent flyers, a wide variety of ages, and 40% men to 60% women. On a scale of "Not nervous at all" to "Slightly Nervous" to "Outright Scared," 52% of respondents indicated they were "Slightly Nervous" or more when they fly.

Think about these results the next time you are on a plane; it is likely that a good percentage of people on that same flight feel the same way you do. Everyone puts on a brave face, don't they? No one wants to lose it on a plane.

You may or may not find comfort in these numbers, but it helps me because there tends to be a stigma about nervous flyers. Flight has evolved over the years from being a glamorous thing for the wealthy into a normalized activity for everyone – like taking a bus or driving a car. For some nervous flyers, admitting your true feelings can be a source of embarrassment.

That said, I've been impressed with the number of public figures over the past few years who have been willing to publicly admit their nervousness about flying.

Typically, they fly a lot, and the average person might not expect them to feel this way. This can help validate some people's feelings and make it more accepted. Public figures who have openly admitted that they are nervous flyers include Oprah Winfrey, Jennifer Aniston, Hope Davis, football commentators Tony Kornheiser and John Madden, and Whoopi Goldberg, just to name a few.

Through my years of people-watching in airports and on planes, it's clear that everyone is trying their best to look calm and collected – myself included. If you saw me on a flight, you would never have guessed the underlying terror I used to feel. This cover-up serves a purpose; I believe that intuitively we know that if one person panics, it can set others into panic as well, and I think we are programmed to try to help each other keep the peace and be brave together.

So remember, you are not alone in your nervousness, and your feelings are not abnormal or silly.

Chapter 2: A Realistic Goal

Unlike some other books, programs, and therapies on the fear of flying, I will be level with you — it is unrealistic that this or any other guidance will totally "cure" your nerves and fears about flying, despite the claims. A FOF class will probably help temporarily – to get you through the next flight..

Instead, the goal is a long-term strategy to not let your nerves or fear *rule* you or prevent you from flying altogether. The goal is to help make you a more willing passenger, by giving you a wide range of real, "field-tested" set of ideas and tools to work with, before and during your flight.

Today, I confidently fly with ease. There are times when I even look forward to it. It took me a while to get to this point, and I still carry my notes (which is now this book) whenever I fly. I know the basics on how flight works, and I don't need or want to know more, because it doesn't change the situation once I'm in the air. I still have a few moments of nerves here and there, but I simply review this book – the things that I have found to work for me, and it helps me get through.

So have a realistic goal – you still might always have some level of nervousness when you fly. But definitely *do all you can* to help yourself, whether it's this book, or a combination of books and resources.

Don't feel helpless about the situation – just the act of trying to empower yourself helps you feel better about this strange quest called flight.

Chapter 3: Let's Be Honest - Flight Is Absurd

I believe that honesty is the best policy... and that if you can admit and appreciate the absurdity of flight, then you can appreciate the "amazingness" of it as well – and develop a greater appreciation for the experience you are about to have.

It helped a lot when I thought through and admitted to myself how I truly felt about flight. Instead of feeling like there was something wrong with me, or just saying, "I'm scared," I dug a little deeper to try to define exactly what it was that made me feel that way. In doing this, I decided that I did not have a "problem" or phobia, and I wasn't going to try to hide my feelings anymore. In doing so, it justified my feelings and that, in turn, helped me appreciate flight even more.

We are fed various messages about flight in our culture – that it should be accepted as just another normal mode of transportation, like getting into a car or on a train. We are fed that fear-of-flying is abnormal – just the fact that the terms "aerophobia" and "aviphobia" exists is proof. We are also fed the idea that flying is good, jet-set, and cool.

But flying is **not** just another kind of transportation. Otherwise there wouldn't be strict standards about who can fly planes, what they can fly, when, and how. There wouldn't be strict standards about airplane inspections and security standards. There wouldn't be whole organizations dedicated to flight and training standards for ground crews, air control tower crews, flight attendants and pilots. There would be only one pilot per flight instead of two or more. So flight is obviously much more than another form of transportation.

Flight is also still a **new** concept. For the huge majority of human existence, human flight did not exist. There were not machines in our skies, and the only human experience of being off the ground was our ability to jump. Only in the last hundred years has the concept of getting into a flying contraption come into existence. And that, in the timespan of human life on earth, is nothing.

To make it even more bizarre, once humans figured out how to fly, it turned into a business. How many people could we put on one of these things, and how often? What could we charge? How could we profit? And thus the passenger flight experience has evolved into what it is today.

To me, the absurdity of flight is this: When you fly, you are sitting in a "giant tin can." You are buckled down in extremely close proximity to a bunch of strangers, and propelled into the air at a speed faster than you'd ever go in your car. You cannot leave. You cannot see what's ahead of you. Your need to pee might be denied at any given moment. You might be jostled around as if you were a kid in a bouncy house. You are subjected to all sorts of strange noises and sensations. There's no way to tell how the flight is going or how the pilots are doing. You are putting your life in the hands of strangers that communicate with you glibly, at the beginning and end of the experience, and most likely only because they are required to do so. You must sit there quietly and wait until it's over. And that's just the flight itself, not to mention all of the pre and post-flight airport hurdles.

I don't write those things to further freak you out; my point is that you already know these things. It's good to articulate how you feel, and I want you to know that *your feelings are justified.* You don't have to call it a "phobia," which is a ridiculous label to begin with, or even "fear-of-flying." You don't have to feel silly about being a nervous flyer.

In fact, I find it strange when someone says they have no anxieties at all about flying, or when they rib me about having been a nervous flyer. Are they in denial, or just don't think about it much, or they have figured out how to enjoy flight, as I have? Whatever it is, my goal as your flight coach is to help you figure out the right mindset that will enable you to fly with ease.

Chapter 4: Flight Is Amazing

As much as I feel flight is absurd, I also believe it is absolutely amazing. I have a deep sense of awe and appreciation about how flight works and the people that envisioned it and made it happen. It is truly incredible, when you stop and really think about it.

It is very possible (and "real") for you to feel two things concurrently about flight – that it is both an absurd *and* amazing. At some of my worst moments in the air, I have been able to turn my perspective around, simply by deciding to *allow* myself to feel the joy of flight. It's simple and true — even the words you use to describe your experience can turn your mood around.

Most nervous flyers are reluctant to allow themselves to feel the joy of flight for fear that they'll be giving in to something... it's almost a superstition. The thinking goes that if you allow yourself to *enjoy* flight, something bad will happen. I'm here to tell you that after over hundreds of flights, taking joy in flight is a good thing, and it's one of the many ways you can cope on your flight.

Instead of saying "I hate flying" or "I'm scared to fly," simply replace it with, "Flying makes me nervous, but it's really amazing." Even if it's forced, just this change of phrasing when thinking or talking about flight can help. It becomes less of the "enemy" and more of a pal (or at least a decent acquaintance!).

Although you may feel like just another passenger, behind the scenes, it is amazing how much is going on to make sure you get from point A to point B with no major issues. Just think of sheer volume of people it takes to make all of this happen — pilots, traffic controllers, flight attendants, baggage handlers, mechanics, airport desk clerks, security agents. It's amazing that it's so coordinated and that it happens at all.

The mental and physical discipline it takes to be a commercial pilot is amazing. I'll bet most commercial pilots don't think twice about it, but if the average person tried it, they would fail.

For pilots, it becomes a job, but it's never a standard fare job like most people have. Pilots know that lives are on the line every day they come to work, including their own, but they don't approach it with the same concerns, nervousness or "What Ifs" that we do – they know, live and breathe that flying is the safest form of transportation in the world.

A pilot's job is exponentially safer than other transportation workers – eg. a bus driver, or taxi driver, or train engineer. They are just as invested as we are in making sure that the planes they are flying that day are working just fine. They want to get home to their families and friends just as much as we passengers do.

If that isn't impressive enough, just think of your alternatives. Just a few short generations ago, your options for travel were a horse-drawn carriage or walking. And even though nowadays you can hop in your car, flight is still much safer and more efficient. I've driven many times from Seattle to San Jose, California — it takes 13.5 hours, without getting out of the car except to pump gas and go to the bathroom (and lots of fast food). A flight for the same distance takes 1.5 hours in the air.

If you can take all of these things in to consideration and transform your negative views into a sense of awe and respect for flight, even if forced or just for a few moments, you can decrease your nervousness. Develop a real appreciation, and try to focus on the wonderment of flight. Make it your friend instead of your enemy. I even go so far as to look at the plane I'm about to fly on in admiration (rather than trepidation) – in the same way that I look at a car that I think is cool-looking.

The next time you step onto a plane, it is okay to acknowledge your initial feelings of being scared or nervous – but acknowledge the amazingness of flight as well. Stating both concepts will serve you well – you don't have to stifle your feelings about it, and you can turn it into a positive statement, which helps calm your nerves.

Chapter 5: Getting To the Heart of the Matter: Why Nervous Flyers Are Nervous

One of the typical things FOF "experts" do is throw numbers at you in the form of statistics, including how much more likely you are to die in some other way, trying to convince you how safe it is to fly. But as a nervous flyer, I always found a few things left unsaid in these approaches. What I wanted to say back is: 1) What's the context – make the numbers more "real," and 2) Despite those statistics, people still die.

Let's tackle #2 first because it's honest and cuts right to the point; it's the gnawing factor for any nervous flyer. The real root of the reason why you don't want to fly is that you don't want to die, and you think that if you get on a plane, it could happen. And you might think it could happen *moreso* than if you were driving your car, because on a plane you have control of nothing, whereas in a car, even as a passenger, you have some degree of control.

Furthermore, dying in an airplane seems incredibly tragic. And the news media makes sure you know about it, too. Even though every day there are awful auto accidents that kill all walks of life and with a frequency much greater than plane crash deaths, these are not covered in any substantial way. If they were covered to the degree plane crashes are, we'd have a nation full of "nervous drivers" and the term "amaxophobia" would be much more prevalent!

Yet every time a commercial flight has a problem, whether an outright crash or other issue that passengers can comment on, you can expect to hear about it in the news for days, if not weeks. It's understandable – because it is such a *rare* occurrence.

If you feel nervous because accidents still occur, it's not because of control issues or some phobia. You're simply normal. I will try to make you feel better about all of this in the next chapter when I cite the odds of this happening to you (incredibly low), but I'm also not going to avoid this topic of what your nervousness is really based in.

Fatalities happen, and although it is extremely rare and the odds of successful flight *are* greatly on your side, all of that logic leaves your brain when you turn on the news and learn about some commercial airline flight tragedy, and probably even moreso when it's a domestic carrier. I know the feelings – the anger, the frustration, sadness and confusion. Why can't flight just be perfect? Why was there a problem? Why do these things still happen? Why can't they just attach giant parachutes to every plane, just in case?

And all of this is amplified when you have an upcoming business trip or vacation flight planned... how can you possibly build yourself up to keep your plans instead of just saying, "I'm never flying again!"

As a reluctant frequent flyer dealing with the news of these rare yet fatal incidents over the years, I've had to climb back up that mountain of courage a few times.

The truth is that there is **no quick fix** for this. You are going to have to build yourself up again in spite of what you have seen and heard about on the news. It takes effort, but you can do it.

Here are a few ways that I personally deal with this situation:

1) First, I purposely ***ignore all stories about fatalities on private/personal*** planes, because although I feel incredibly sorry for the people on board and their families, private flight is not as regulated and controlled as commercial flight. Just about anyone can get a pilot's license for a private plane (much to my dismay, but that is a different book altogether) and there is often 1 pilot instead of 2. And many of these flights do not have the full resources of Air Traffic Control and equipment like commercial flights do, many relying on visual abilities only. I never fly private planes and I don't focus on private plane incidents.

2) If the tragedy revolves around a commercial flight, I ***review the story, but don't dwell on it***. What I mean by dwell is – I don't purposely read or listen to more than the first burst of news I've seen on it, including the speculation on how it happened. I say a prayer for the victims and their families, and then I **steer clear** of all TV and internet news outlets for a few days and allow myself to go into a black hole. Denial? You bet — but I like to think of it more as my survival instinct... if I have to fly soon, I

simply don't need the constant reminder. The more you are reminded of it, the more you will think about it. They never figure out the *real* reason for the incident quickly anyway (it's all just speculation from various talking heads), so why focus on it?

3) I ***don't focus on the type of jet*** it was because all jets have been in accidents, yet all types have also had millions of successful flights as well. Planes are incredibly tested in adverse conditions, reviewed, and continuously improved.

4) To ***build my courage back up and get some perspective***, I start by re-reading the "Making the Numbers Real" chapter followed by the rest of this book. I think about the thousands upon thousands of successful flights that happened that day, and will happen tomorrow, and the next day, and the day after that... and so on.

5) For my pending flight, I ***develop a very proactive vision and attitude*** that nothing will go wrong. Imagine if you just ***knew*** that your flight was going to be okay – you would be so incredibly relaxed and not even worry about it.

6) I remind myself that the ***frequency of these incidents decreases while the frequency of flight increases all the time***, and so feel grateful for how lucky I am to experience flying nowadays vs. 20 – 30 years ago.

7) I have a ***belief system*** about death, which is basically that I don't get to choose my time to go, or the how, or the why. I'm not asking you

to believe the same thing; I'm just saying what works for me. When I view it from this angle, it helps me gain perspective that it's not in my control anyway, so it's futile to even worry about it.

8) I ***ask for help from my family and friends***. I let them know I am flying soon and that I could use any words of encouragement and their perspective in light of the recent tragedy. If I could loan out my mom to you, she would look at you funny and say something like, "Don't be ridiculous. You can't let fear rule your life!" There's nothing like the "snap out of it!" advice from good ol' Mom.

9) I ***don't pressure myself.*** If a recent tragic incident has really affected me, I allow myself an out (to not go). In reality, in 20 years of frequent flying, there's only been one time where I changed my mind. I have otherwise always carried on with my plans. Yet just the simple act of respecting myself — just in acknowledging that I have a ***choice*** on whether or not to fly – is empowering.

That's all I can give you on the "people still die" thing. It takes time and courage to build yourself back up; it's a choice only you can make, but it's worth it. Keep reading because the next chapter might help you gain greater perspective as well.

Chapter 6: Comfort in Numbers

Citing statistics on the safety of flight is a common technique to help nervous flyers; some do find "comfort in numbers." What I've tried to add is some perspective to help make these numbers feel a bit more real. I recommend looking at the numbers as just one of many things to help you think about flight.

When you really stop and think about it, it's rather incredible that flight has far surpassed other forms of transportation in terms of safety, speed and convenience.

How many flights are there?

In 2008 alone, there were over 21 *million* flight departures worldwide of commercial jets (eg. passenger, cargo) except military use, accounting for over 46 million flight hours[2]. Stop and think about this for a minute...

21 million departing flights in a year means that an average of 57,500 flights took off per *day* around the world. That's an average of 2,395 flights taking off per *hour*. In the last *minute* that just occurred as you were reading this, an average of 40 new flights of commercial jets just took off.

Odds are you've been to a stadium before, at least once in your life. So picture a big stadium — for example, the new Yankee Stadium seats over 52,000. Imagine a full stadium of 52,000 people, and you're sitting there looking around, surrounded by a sea of people just in your section and level alone. Now imagine that each person in that entire stadium represents a flight taking off. This large stadium full of people represents the number of flights that take off in *one day alone* (actually, there are more!)

Picture that stadium full of people again, and then picture two stadiums full of people right next to each other. Then 10 stadiums. Then 20, then 100... that's right, 100 stadiums full of people. Then make it 200. Then 300. Then throw in nearly another 100. Picture almost 400 very full stadiums next to each other. Every single person in all of these stadiums represents one flight. That's how many flights take off in just in one year alone.

Picture an image of the earth from space, but with the ability to see airplanes flying through the air at any given moment. You would see a swarm of airplanes flying around, all over the world (and that doesn't even include private planes, like corporate services or personal planes). Again, an average of 57,500 planes in the air in one day... millions of people – pilots, flight crew, passengers zig-zagging across the earth at any moment in time.

Now think about every day that goes by that you *don't* hear about a commercial plane crash in the news. That means there has been an average of 57,500 successful commercial flights that day. That is incredible!

Another angle is to consider also how many daily flights some US-based carriers offer (according to their websites): United – nearly *3000* flights daily. Southwest - over *3,300* flights daily. Delta – almost *6000* flights daily. So just for these 3 US airlines, that is **12,000** flights **every single day** of the year.

Let's say each flight has an average of 100 passengers (a combination of larger jets and commuter jets – for example, a Boeing 737 can hold 180 – 215 seats depending on configuration). So that's an average of over **1.2 million people** that successfully get from point A to point B successfully every single day, just on these 3 airlines alone.

So to say that **millions of passengers** have **successful** flights **every day** just on US-based carriers alone is no exaggeration.

Your Odds of Success

Your odds of making it on a flight are incredible, which is why I always keep the following catchphrase in my mind – "Flying is the safest form of transportation in the world." In moments of ongoing turbulence, or a steep landing, that's what pops into my head, and it helps me get through the moment, because it's true.

The US Department of Transportation[3] confirms this; the "Deaths Per Year" by transportation mode goes in this order (most to least): Motor Vehicles, Motorcycles, Railroads, Bicycles, Air Carriers. The number of people that die per year in motor vehicles is approximately the same as the state with the largest population – California (over 36,000).

The DOT also lists that the "General Population Risk Per Year" odds of dying in a car is 1 out of 7,700. Envision that large stadium again; this means that about 1 out of every 7 people you see sitting around you in ***one*** stadium alone are going to die in a motor vehicle accident in one year. (Depressing, isn't it?) In an air carrier, the odds are 1 out of 2,067,000. That means 1 person out of almost ***40 full*** stadiums.

Using the Numbers

If you were a Vulcan (from Star Trek) and used only logic to decide how to look at things, you would find it ridiculous to even worry or have any fear on a flight — because your odds of dying by other means are so much greater, and the risk in flight is entirely insignificant. You are far more likely to die not only from other forms of transportation, but also from cardiovascular disease, a tornado, getting hit by lightening, or via bee sting.

Odds are you're not a Vulcan (although pretending to be one on a flight is a decent coping technique!), and so the logic only goes so far. So to make all of this information useful, I encourage you to find simple but impactful summary statements about these numbers that appeal to both your logic *and* emotion. Then repeat them in your moment of need. The ones that work best for me are:

1) Flying is the safest form of transportation in the world.
2) An average of 57,500 flights occur successfully each day.
3) Several million people fly safely to their destination, every single day of the year.

Chapter 7: Why Bother Flying, Anyway?

Many nervous-to-petrified flyers don't even bother flying at all... just the thought of having to take a flight makes them queasy. But some things are enough to motivate even the most freaked-out flyer to step on that plane.

As your flight coach, I encourage you to use these reminders when you are asking yourself at any point, *why am I doing this?*

> **Fly for family and friends**: Don't let your nervousness about flying come before your family and friends! If you miss someone, or if someone misses you and they're brave enough to say it or even hint at it, then go. And sometimes the only way to go is through flight.
>
> You have this one life, and the best way to navigate through it and appreciate it is by staying connected to the people that love and/or care about you. You can't hug and get that miraculous eye contact over the webcam, phone, texting, or email. Those things are nice, yes, and better than nothing. But they are second-rate to being there in-person.
>
> If you don't go, you will likely regret it later in life. Cultivating and cherishing your family and friends is the most important thing in the world. It's more important than working, watching TV, reading a book, redecorating your house, shopping, and many other things.

I'll say it another way because it's so important: Don't let your nervousness about flying ***take priority*** over your family and friends! If you don't go, that is exactly what you're doing. It is, in a way, selfish on your part.

Fly for Work: Don't let your nervousness about flying come before being successful at your job. If you're asked to travel somewhere, it's for a reason. You may or may not agree with that reason, but your boss doesn't care... they have a purpose in mind. And let's look at the alternatives: you could make up a story on why you can't go and your boss could buy it, but after the second or third time, they'll just think you're insubordinate.

You could offer to drive instead of fly, but if it's far away, your boss will likely look at you as if you've lost your mind, not to mention you are taking away days of productivity. Or you could simply confess your feelings about flying, but if you do this, be sure you have taken a job where it's very clear that ***no*** travel is expected. It is not fair to take a job where any travel is required and then not follow through when asked.

Fly for vacation: I'll bet there are plenty of great vacation spots within a reasonable driving distance from where you live. That's nice, but it's likely that one of these days you'll want to branch out a little, and you probably don't have enough vacation days to drive across the country and back just to visit our nation's capitol, or look out over the Grand Canyon, or see the wonders of Yosemite, or visit the Alamo. You can choose to put these things off until you retire and do have the time to drive, but, let's get real – you may or may not have the stamina or savings to do those things at age 65 or 70, and the time is *now*.

If you have a family, whether it's just a spouse or you also have kids, you need to realize that you are acting selfishly when you come up with a "vacation" to the local water park for the third summer in a row. Prioritize your family's needs on this one. While traveling by car or RV can be a great experience for kids, your destinations are as limited as your vacation time. Optimize your time off for you and your family.

Also, try not to pass on your nervousness to your kids. When I had my son, although by then I was at ease when I flew, I vowed to become even moreso — extremely relaxed — while flying, even while he was a baby. Now that he is almost 3, it's more critical than ever that I tap into my sense of adventure and fun during flight so that he does not pick up on any nervousness. It has been a great practice for me to be totally relaxed during a flight – something I would never have thought possible during my initial nervous flying years.

Give your kids the gift of a sense of adventure! Be brave and fearless!

Fly if you don't like driving (or can't drive): I love driving so I can't relate to this "reason to fly" — but there are millions of people who do not enjoy driving the way I do. So this is one of the main reasons for people to fly instead of drive. Why spend 5 days crossing the country when you could spend 5 hours in the air instead?

Fly for safety: Even if you do enjoy driving as much as I do, the statistics are unquestionable. It's *always* safer to fly to your destination than by car… even in the middle of a huge storm! Remember those odds in the "Making the Numbers Real" chapter. Flight is by far the safest form of transportation in the world.

Chapter 8: Control What You Can

I have always found it amusing when nervous flyers are told they have "control issues" as if it's a problem or irrational. And some might theorize "Well, we never really have control over anything," but that's not totally true. Proportionally, you *do* give up a lot more control when you fly compared to other forms of transportation. It's simply a fact; not some abnormal feeling to have or try to hide.

You can use this fact to your advantage, though, and focus on controlling what you can:

1) The first step is to simply acknowledge that you lose some control. Many people have a hard time saying this, and instead cite the aspects of flight that bothers them, like "I don't like turbulence" or take-off, etc. But the fact is that if they felt that they had even *some* control over these things, they would feel a lot better about it. So just acknowledge that you are going to be giving up some of your control during the flight process.

2) Let's look at all of the things you *do* have control over:
   a) Whether or not to fly in the first place. Taking a flight is ultimately your decision; no one can make you do it. You might *think* they do (eg. a spouse or friend or boss) but ultimately no one can force you to step on to a plane. It is your choice.

b) Your choice of airline and general time of day that you fly. And to some degree, your seat.

c) Your preparation, including making sure the right things are in your Carry-On bag (Chapter 15).

d) Your level of courage, mental preparation and general attitude.

e) Your activities on the flight (within limits).

f) Your ability to ask for information or get help from the flight crew.

g) Your response to stress.

You can do a lot with the things on this list. Throughout this book, you'll find ways to optimize each of these things that you have control over.

3) Realize the power you have to minimize the potential of other stressors that can come up in the flight experience. Examples of additional stressors are delays, food and beverage service issues (or costs), ongoing turbulence that doesn't allow you to get up from your seat, who you sit next to, and more. As a nervous flyer, the last thing you want to do is add more stress to yourself.

For example, if turbulence makes you nervous, imagine also being hungry and thirsty while the food service is delayed. Or let's say the part your dread the most is take-off, but your flight is delayed on the runway for an hour, and you didn't bring enough to keep yourself occupied, so your anxiety level goes through the roof. Or imagine that you are wore flip flops on the flight, only to find your feet are freezing, with all of the blankets already in use.

There is absolutely **no reason** for you to end up in situations like this. You can minimize the impact of these additional stressors through preparation (which is the focus of the "Preparing to Fly" section of this book). Even if you are the type to not do much planning ahead, now is the time. It's a simple decision to make — if doing all you can do to minimize your anxiety is important to you, you need to prepare, both mentally and with having the right things on hand.

Chapter 9: People Do This for a Living

Another perspective on flight that I find useful is to remind myself that people actually fly for a living. Just like most people go to work every day to earn money, so do pilots and flight attendants. In the US and Canadian airlines alone, there are over 53,000 pilots[4] that belong to the Airline Pilots Association, the largest airline pilot union in the world, plus nearly 100,000 flight attendants.

This is their job. It's normal to them. Taking off, cruising at altitude, turbulence, descending, landing – they do it all the time, sometimes several times a week depending on their assignments (domestic or overseas). Even in bad turbulence where the pilot asks the flight attendants to be seated, it's routine to them.

You, on the other hand, just see them once – on your flight. But that same person flying that plane or getting your drink has probably flown thousands of miles and interacted with hundreds if not thousands of passengers just ***in that week alone***.

Why would anyone sign up for a job like this if they were nervous about flying? Maybe it's because they're not; they have no doubt that flying is the safest form of transportation. And that what goes on behind the scenes – work done by the mechanics, air traffic controllers, and more must be good, because they keep doing it. They want to live, and they don't think they're going to die when they go to work.

When you're feeling nervous on a flight, look at your flight crew if at all possible, and ponder the moment from their perspective. And keep in mind that if they look stressed or tense during turbulence or some other part of the flight, it's probably due to something entirely different than what *you* are stressed about – after all, they feel turbulence all the time. Maybe they just remembered something to add to their to-do list, or their stomach is growling. Maybe they're annoyed because it's harder to not spill drinks while serving passengers during turbulence. Perhaps they can't believe so many people still aren't buckled back up even though they've been asked to, or they don't want to bump their own heads. It's business as usual for them – all in a day's work.

Chapter 10: It's Temporary

Another good way to think about flight is to keep reminding yourself that "it's temporary." It sounds so simple, but it's powerful, and it's brought me comfort at some of my most nervous moments, because I know that what I'm experiencing will be over with at some point. It may or may not be ***as soon*** as I want it to, but, it ***will*** be over with.

It works because part of what makes people nervous is the concern that the discomfort or unpleasantness they are facing will continue, when they just want it to stop. You want the turbulence to stop; you want the take-off to get over with, you don't want to fly over water, etc. Or you at least want some idea or reassurance of when it will stop so that you can try to relax again.

Unfortunately, the pilots often don't convey detailed information during the flight. They are working, and not here to give you the play-by-play of the flight (as much as I wish they would – I'd even advocate for "pilot-cams"). What ***does*** work for me though is to simply say, "This <phase> is temporary. The whole flight is temporary. This phase of the flight that's bothering me ***will*** end, and this plane will land, and I will be on to my next thing."

Even if you think you already know this inherently, I encourage you to actually say it, and very matter-of-factly, during your next most trying moment on a flight. If you can't say it aloud under your breath for concern of being heard, write it down, and as many times as feels convincing. It could bring instant perspective and a degree of relaxation, because it's true. The way you are feeling *is* fleeting in the grand scheme of things. You can and should look forward to the next thing.

Chapter 11: Put Fear in Perspective

Nervousness or fear is not an unhealthy thing at times; but our goal is to manage it effectively so that it doesn't overwhelm you. This again is why I say "beware" when other FOF books or programs promise to "eliminate your fear." Instead, set the goal to "manage" your nervousness or fear – which will in turn reduce it and put you more at ease.

One way of managing your fear is to keep it in perspective – both in terms of defining it and putting it up against a larger scale. The famous Franklin Roosevelt quote, "There's nothing to fear but fear itself" makes the point — if you focus on your fear, it just grows larger and larger.

At the airport and on the plane, I think about that quote, but also other "things to fear" compared to flying. When you stop and really think about it, aren't there many other things to be *more* afraid of than a form of transportation that is successful for millions of people every single day? It is also a good idea to look at flying in terms of the actual frequency that this fear is real for you —usually only as frequently as you fly.

A perspective statement I use throughout the flight process, from being in the airport to landing, is "This is nothing compared to... (fill in the blank)."

To finish this statement for yourself, think outside of yourself a bit and compare flying to other scary or super-challenging things that other people face - eg.

"This is nothing compared to what our soldiers face in the line of fire," or "This is nothing compared to being homeless," or "This is nothing compared to what Christopher Reeve went through" – hopefully you get the point.

If it helps to make it more personal, think of a greater challenge **you** have overcome, whether it was circumstantial, medical, or anything else, and recognize what was truly harder... that or getting through a 5-hour flight once in a while? One of my personal favorites is: "Getting through this flight is **nothing** compared to giving birth to a 10.5 lb posterior-facing baby girl!"

I think of this technique as "a slap upside the head" and I use it a lot. It really helps to remind yourself that while your nervousness about flight is real and legitimate, but when compared to other things it can become less overwhelming.

Chapter 12: A Spiritual Experience

If you are spiritual or religious at all, taking a flight is an incredible opportunity to feel closer to God, or your guardian angels, or whatever your belief may be. For many, flying is a huge leap of faith, and often the ability to do that comes from having faith in something larger than yourself.

Being spiritual or religious is a great foundation to find your own inner strength and confidence to get through the flight experience. Pray for the strength and courage to take this flight, know that you are not alone, and be grateful for the gift of your bravery.

And pray not just for your own safety, but also in graciousness and gratitude that people were inspired to create this experience in the first place. And for the flight crew, that they are taking joy in their work, and that you are doing what you can to help them and others on the flight.

A wonderful spiritual experience that flight brings is just the view from above – the planet itself, the sky, the sun and the moon – being able to see these from "God's perspective" can help change your perspective too. I encourage you to bring reading materials that will help remind you of your faith – again because when you feel nervous, it is harder to recall things as easily as when you're relaxed.

SECTION 2: PREPARING TO FLY

My motto for this section is "the more you are prepared, the less you will be scared." Mental and physical preparation are key in your ability to manage your flight, and perhaps even enjoy it. Don't take the approach of purchasing the ticket and then living with dread until the day arrives. Proactively help yourself – it will make a difference.

Chapter 13: Selecting a Carrier

To purchase tickets, I tend to either use the airline's site, or an online tool that pools several options together for you to choose from, like expedia.com. If you are a new flyer and unsure about what you're doing, a travel agent can be a great help. You are their customer, so don't be shy about asking questions and having them walk you through every detail. A good travel agent should also be able to recommend resources for nervous flyers.

I am a little biased when it comes to which airlines and types of airplanes I'll fly on. I'll give you my opinions and preferences, which are just that. No one is paying me to call out their companies (believe me, I could use the money, but it's just not the case!). So I write the following in the spirit of totally unscientific, totally biased personal preferences only:

- **Carriers for domestic trips:** I will use pretty much any *major* US carrier. I do tend to use Southwest Airlines the most because they fly to many of the places I tend to go, and I like their frequent flyer program. They have also had very few safety issues and fly only Boeing 737s. I like the idea that all of their mechanics and pilots are focused on one type of jet, and so I rationalize that there's less chance of screwing anything up. (Plus I think it is a smart business strategy.) But I have also had plenty of perfectly safe and smooth travels on United, Alaska, Delta, Continental, USAir, American, Hawaiian, ATA, and more. If you really want to dig, you can find safety ratings for various airlines on the internet. But I caution you – these types of sites can do more harm than good for some nervous flyers!

- **Carriers for international trips:** I stick to the major airlines only, and I prefer United, British Airways and Delta. If needed, I will pay more for these tickets because my peace of mind is worth it. Even if it was for work and the travel agent said I needed to take a different (foreign) carrier because it was cheaper, I would talk to my boss and offer to personally pay the difference in airfare. *Nothing* is worth more than my peace of mind when it comes to flying overseas.

- **I try to avoid small planes** unless there is no other choice. I feel so brave for flying in the first place... I don't need to put myself through more stress by going on anything smaller than a 737. I've done it a few times and actually had decent experiences (and will only do so through major carriers). But I've also heard the horror stories about excessive turbulence and so forth. If I fly to a location that requires a small plane, I'll rent a car instead. My personal threshold is 6 hours. If it's going to take me more than 6 hours by car from the airport to my final destination, then I'll do the small plane. (Or if there are particularly hazardous road conditions along the way).

- **If I am most concerned with arriving on time,** I choose the earliest morning flight out.

- **However, I prefer night flights.** It's just a preference, but I've noticed that I am calmer, my fellow passengers seem to be a bit more relaxed, I can have a glass of wine, and I enjoy looking at the evening and night sky. However, choose evening/night flights only if you are willing to be a little late to your destination (not always the case, but more likely). Morning flights tend to be more on time, in my experience.

Note: I don't advocate that nervous flyers drink alcohol on a plane, but if you do, limit it to one serving. Drinking more actually causes more agitation and anxiety for the average person (more on this in Chapter 28).

Chapter 14: Seat Selection

Window or Aisle?

Unless you already know for certain that you prefer a window seat, I highly recommend that nervous flyers try for an aisle seat. Most airlines will let you select your seat ahead of time, either through an online tool, or, you might have to call. However, the earlier you book, the better your chances, because aisle seats always book first.

Here are some pros and cons to window vs. aisle, based on my own experience.

Window seats are great if you want to see where you are at in the flight process or how far you are from the ground. They're also good if you to be able to close the window shade (this might not make you popular with the other people in your aisle, but, the window seat owner always seems to rule the window either way, I've noticed).

However, if you want to minimize the constant reminder that you're on an airplane and high above the ground, don't choose a window seat. Even if you can close the shade during flight, they require you to keep it open during take-off and landing, and those are often the most nerve-wracking parts for nervous flyers. Plus, it is a lot harder for the average-sized adult to access your Carry-On bag stowed under the seat in front of you.

Aisle seats are great because if you need to take a break and collect yourself in the bathroom (or actually have to go!), you are not "stuck" and having to beg and/or climb over your fellow passengers to get by. If you ever feel the slightest bit claustrophobic, always choose an aisle seat. Aisle seats allow for better stretching of the legs, and a better view of what's going on inside the plane in terms of when drinks or food are coming, what the flight attendants are doing or reacting to, and you can usually immediately stand all the way up after the flight is over.

Also, it is much easier to access your Carry-On bag stowed under the seat in front of you if you are in an aisle seat. Finally, aisle seats let you better able to focus on other things besides the flight; if you can't see the wing, you are less likely to obsess over it, for example.

Middle seats are to be avoided, unless you are sitting next to a loved one. Always try to book well in advance to avoid middle seats... you don't need that kind of added misery. If traveling on an airline that does not do seat assignments, always use the online tools to check in the day before the flight (usually allowed 24 hours prior to the flight time). Even if you don't have a printer, just check in online to secure a good place for boarding, and you can print the actual ticket when you arrive at the airport.

Front or Back?

Theories abound as to the safest part of the plane (front or back), and I've even heard things like "you feel the turbulence more in the back of the plane." But in my experience, the differences are not noticeable.

The approach I take and advocate for any nervous flyer is simply to sit as close as you can to ***exit doors,*** which means the very front, the middle, or the very back. Even though in over 20 years of frequent flying I've not had one emergency incident, it just makes me feel better to know that should anything ever happen, I would be close to the exit doors. So that means I either:

1) Shell out money for a first-class ticket to be in the front of the plane (if you can afford it or have earned enough frequent flyer points to do it – it's worth it for the nervous flyer!)
2) Call the airline or arrive at the airport really early and see if I can get an exit row seat (middle of the plane) – great extra leg room but usually doled out to frequent flyers. If I can't get in the actual exit row, I try to sit as close as possible.
3) Sit in the back (I do this when traveling with my kids).

Chapter 15: Your Top 10 Carry-On Essentials

As a nervous flyer, preparing your smaller Carry-On is one of **the** most critical parts of the flight process. I want you to spend **as much time as possible** planning for what's in your smaller Carry-On bag, and as much in advance as possible. Because what you bring on the plane can make or break your trip.

Our goal is to minimize any **additional** stressors in the time window of your flight. If you are already anxious about flying, there is no need to add any additional anxiety, which can happen if you're not prepared.

Usually you are allowed to have two Carry-Ons – one average-sized backpack or purse-type bag (that can fit under the seat), plus one small suitcase or duffel bag (most people use rolling bags). The one I want you to focus on is your **smaller bag**, because your larger bag could be sent to luggage if the overhead bins are starting to fill up. I have had this happen to me and seen this happen to others many, many times.

So have the following things accessible in your **smaller bag** that can fit under your seat – and make sure it includes at least **all ten things** in the list below, if not more!

If you have difficulty envisioning how you can cram these 10+ things into your smaller Carry-On, I recommend you use a good quality **travel-oriented** (vs. school-oriented) backpack rather than, say, a large tote bag or purse. (In fact, I always put my purse contents in my travel backpack, and then pack my purse in my large suitcase. Dealing with a purse in addition to Carry-Ons is not efficient.)

One important note: Activities you normally find to be enjoyable and inconsequential in your regular life, for example intense or dramatic movies or reading the newspaper may seem like a good idea for a plane ride. However, these things are likely causing you minor stress, even if you don't know it. The difference is that while undue stress from any of these things is probably not even noticeable to you in normal life, they *are* more likely to affect your mood in a flight if you are already nervous to begin with.

For example, your adrenaline normally goes up when you watch those actions flicks in your home, but how will that adrenaline affect you when you're stuck on a plane for another two hours? That deep, sad song you love so much normally makes you feel melancholy, but for a nervous flyer in a flight, you don't need any sad feelings to stick to you and perpetuate. So please, take my word for it, and follow the guidance below. (If traveling with kids, see additional essentials in Chapter 36.)

TOP 10 CARRY-ON ESSENTIALS CHECKLIST

Your BRING Checklist:	Why this is so important:
1) This book	This book is your portable flight coach! If you're nervous and need help remembering coping techniques, they're all right in here. Purposely designed for your moment of need, small and discreet and with blank notes pages... it's here to help.
2) At least one picture of your loved ones (family, friends) in **paper** form (**don't** rely on your cell phone or laptop). Preferably, several photos!	Focusing on a loved one and actually being able to see them visually provides instant comfort as well as distraction. Pull out this picture(s) before the flight takes off, during take-off, in flight as needed, and at landing. No matter what you are feeling, it will likely draw a smile to your face, and help you feel determined to get through the flight.
3) Something funny that always makes you smile, again in paper form: A favorite comic, humor book, short story, quote(s)	Relief through humor is one of the best ways to cope with any nervous feelings. Arm yourself with things that make you laugh, whether inside or out loud. Make sure this thing is accessible at any time (does not require an electronic device to use) so that you can refer to it during take-off and landing.

Your BRING Checklist:	Why this is so important:
4) Bottled water (ensure enough time to buy this at the airport after you get through the Security line)	I'm always surprised how people rely on the "food & beverage service" on flights rather than come prepared. If your goal is to minimize the amount of worry you have about anything while on a flight, then this is a no-brainer, even if you don't normally drink a lot of water. Don't ever depend on the food and beverage service – always bring your own. And drinking water (even if you are also drinking other things) is essential to staying hydrated, not to mention the great feeling of relief you'll have should your flight get delayed.
5) Two snacks per every hour of your flight even if you don't normally eat that much (eg. granola, protien or even candy bars; peanuts, sustainable and easy to prepare fruits like an apple, box of raisins, or a banana; chip mixes)	Following on the same theme as above – minimize the possibility of worry or panic when you realize that the flight doesn't even offer food service (more and more common these days), or charges $5 – $10 for a little sandwich with some chips. And again, even with great service and clear skies, you could get delayed at any time. Never take this chance – stock up! The worst that could happen is that you have some extra snack food at your destination!

Your BRING Checklist:	Why this is so important:
6) Two magazines or book of easy games (eg. crosswords or soduku), or other form of written entertainment per every hour of your flight, even if you don't think you'll actually read them	For nervous flyers, magazines are the best way to stay "lite" in your thinking and distracted, since each page is different. It is always a good idea to have a few with you just in case one of them is not grabbing your attention, and again to help manage your feelings during flight delays. Brain challenge puzzles are a great way to engage your mind as well. Just make sure these are easy puzzles so that you avoid frustration – the last feeling you want to have if you are a nervous flyer! Now is not the time to try to take your skills up a notch with a big challenge. Books are fine but – I have "rules" about them for planes – in the "Optional But Advised" section coming up.

Your BRING Checklist:	Why this is so important:
7) Any medications your normally take, even if your flight is not during the time you normally take them, plus basic headache or cold medicine	Don't rely on your flight to be timely, ever. Although most of the time you arrive when estimated, flight delays can happen at any time for a variety of reasons, even in the best of weather. Don't heap additional stress on to yourself by only packing any medications into your checked-in luggage. Bring them with you in your smallest bag, always! As for basic over-the-counter headache or cold medicine, no, your flight attendants don't neces-sarily have this stuff handy, and even if they do, they might not legally be able to give it to you. So always bring what you normally use for headaches or minor aches and pains. There are no restrictions on med-ications in Carry-Ons in US air-ports, but if you want reassurance, you can look it up at tsa.gov.

Your BRING Checklist:	Why this is so important:
8) Noise-reducing headphones or earplugs	A good set of noise-reducing headphones, although costly, are a great investment, even if you don't fly much. First, it's a great way to tune out some of the noises of the plane that you might find anxiety-producing; you can wear them during take-off as long you're not plugged into anything. Second, you have no control over who you sit near on a flight – a loud toddler, a chatty neighbor, a crying baby… depending on how you feel about these situations, headphones can help cancel out noise, or send a message that you're not looking for a discussion.
9) Your Purpose Statement and Courage Quotes	See the next Chapter (16) "Must-Do Mental Preparation" for how to create your Purpose Statement and Courage quotes. Then write them down, bring them with you and ensure they're easily accessible. I advise you write these directly in this book (using the notes pages in the back).

Your BRING Checklist:	Why this is so important:
10) Pen or Pencil, tablet and/or greeting cards	Writing is a great way to keep your mind busy in flight. There are many things you can write on a plane: to-do lists, to-get lists, letters, thank-you notes, ideas, poems, etc. You can use a laptop or other device instead, but again old fashioned pencil and paper is optimal because you can use them during take-off and landing, or if your laptop battery decides to give up.
Optional But Advised:	
Thank You Notes	A few years ago, I started the practice of writing Thank You notes on flights. Getting "out of your head" and feeling grateful can work wonders. Write to family and friends for various reasons – it doesn't have to be for gifts – it can be for any nice deed. I also like to write a Thank You note to the flight crew. I tell them how appreciative I am of the work they do, and for getting me from point A to point B safely. This is a great way for a nervous flyer to focus on the amazement of flight and feel appreciative of what the flight crew does for a living.

Your BRING Checklist:	Why this is so important:
Optional But Advised:	
Music player (and ensure your noise-reducing headphones are compatible)	Music, in addition to magazines and games, is a great way to tune into the positive and keep any negative or nervous feelings at bay. However, you need to pick music that is either inspiring or relaxing, vs. songs that are either depressing or frenetic. Look at your favorite playlists and create your "feel-good" playlist. There is also a "Top Flight Songs" suggested play list in Chapter 34 that I have formed over the years. Be sure to fully charge your music player the night before your flight.
Movie player, favorite movies (and ensure your noise-reducing headphones are compatible)	Don't rely on long flights to have movies you want to see (and don't rely on shorter flights to have movies at all). If you want to watch movies in flight, always be prepared and bring your own. I recommend comedies and feel-good movies only. Even if you love a great drama, action or horror flick, a flight might not be the time for it, if you're already anxious. Plus, you should be respectful of the person sitting next to you, who is inevitably going to see and likely hear your movie to some degree. Be sure to fully charge your movie player the night before your flight.

Your BRING Checklist:	Why this is so important:
Optional But Advised:	
Novels or other books	Books are a gamble because unless you are familiar enough with the author, you could find yourself in a bad book getting bored very quickly, as I learned on a long flight from San Francisco to Sydney. If you try a book, go with something generally uplifting, or re-read a favorite book. A flight is not the time to read anything that is depressing or has the potential to add more stress to a nervous flyer.
Not Advised:	
Newspapers (or if so, skip depressing articles)	Newspapers are popular sellers at airports but, again I argue that for a nervous flyer, a flight is not the time and place for them. It takes just one bad article to get your head in a negative place, when we want you to stay as upbeat as possible during your journey. Newspapers are full of depressing stories, so why risk it? Take a break - the news will always be there for you when you land.

Your BRING Checklist:	Why this is so important:
Not Advised:	
Total reliance on electronic gadgets for entertainment...	I love technology and although I suggest several forms of it above under "Optional But Advised," I want you to avoid **total** reliance on it when you fly. The first reason is because you cannot use electronic devices during the typically most stressful periods of the flight. You need to have accessible things to help you in those times. The other reason to not count on electronic devices is "just in case." Just in case you bring the DVDs but forget the player (or vice versa). Or as I have experienced, just in case your fully charged DVD player decides to stop working for no logical reason. Or just in case your music player loses all of its charge because you didn't realize it was accidentally on since yesterday. Or you forget the headphones, or you accidentally drop it and it breaks, etc. You get the point!

Finally, don't give yourself extra anxiety by waiting until the last minute to pack your Carry-On bag. Get it out *at least a week before you fly,* and put things in there gradually. Every time you add something to your bag, I want you to think positively about your flight – even something simple like, "I'm going to have a great flight."

Chapter 16: Must-Do Mental Preparation

The following 4 steps are crucial for nervous flyers. The week before your flight, you might be tempted to do all you can to block out the fact that you'll have to fly soon, but *do the following 4 things anyway.* They will help you go into your flight with less anxiety. Arm yourself with confidence, even if it feels forced! It can make a big difference.

There are four specific mental preparation activities I want you to do the Week Before: 1) Develop a Statement of Purpose, 2) "What If" Management, 3) Courage Quotes, and 4) Seeing Your Success.

1) Purpose Statement

What is the purpose of your flight? Whatever it is, create and write down a positive "Purpose Statement" (I suggest using the Notes pages in this book), and then I want you to add my "safety statement" to the end of it (see below). Then read it every day. Even if you don't want to think about your flight, *do this anyway.*

This step is important because if your purpose is clear, positive, and firmly planted in your brain, it will be less daunting when you're actually on the flight, and, it will be easily accessible in your mind during your moments of need. It only takes a minute a day to read your Purpose Statement. I don't care when or in what setting — just do it!

I've written out some sample Purpose Statements below based on some of the most common reasons people fly, but if they don't work for you, use your own! It is most effective if you use your own voice and it resonates with you.

The "safety statement" I want you to add at the end of your statement is: "… and flying is the safest form of transportation in the world." Add this even if you don't think it's true, because you need to hear it (and it *is* true!).

Sample Purpose Statements:

> **Flying for family and friends**: The purpose of my flight is to be with my family and/or friends (insert names here). I have this one life, and the most important thing is to stay connected to the people that love and care about me, and that means more than the phone or webcam. I refuse to let my nervousness block me from this trip, and the best way to optimize my time with (names) is by flying. I can't wait to see them. And thank goodness I am flying, because flying is the safest form of transportation in the world.

> **Fly for work:** The purpose of my flight is for work. My work is important to me because it lets me live my life well and pay the bills. My work would not fund and ask me to go on this trip if they did not feel it was important. I refuse to let my nervousness block me from this trip and success at work, and the best way to opti-

mize my personal time is by flying. And thank goodness I am flying, because flying is the safest form of transportation in the world.

Fly for vacation: The purpose of my flight is to have a nice vacation. I have this one life, and it is important to nurture myself with some fun and relaxation. I refuse to let my nervousness block me (and my family) from this trip, and the best way to optimize my time on vacation is by flying. I can't wait to get there. And thank goodness I am flying, because flying is the safest form of transportation in the world.

Fly if you don't like driving (or can't drive): The purpose of my flight is simply because I don't like to or can't take some other form of transportation instead. By flying I get to optimize my time for myself, and I'm going to make the best of it. And thank goodness I am flying, because flying is the safest form of transportation in the world.

2) "What If" Management

Nervous flyers tend to be full of the "What Ifs," as I used to be. These insidious little thoughts can build quickly and take your anxiety level through the roof before a flight.

The goal is to take your "What Ifs" and convert them to better statements. ***Don't underestimate the power of this little trick***, even if it sounds trite or forced. You can use this throughout your whole experience from pre-flight, in-flight to post-flight.

First, you have to learn to recognize your What Ifs. Since they're usually just in your head, you might not always say the actual words "What If," but if you really try, you will start to see your patterns. Here are some typical What If statements:

- WHAT IF the plane crashes?
- WHAT IF the wings fall off?
- WHAT IF the pilot makes a mistake?

And the What Ifs can be more subtle too... eg. in the form of statements vs. questions, such as:

- My luggage will be lost. (Which is really: "WHAT IF my luggage gets lost?")
- I'll be a nervous wreck. (Which is really: "WHAT IF I am so nervous I'll lose it in front of everyone?")
- I can't believe I have to do this! (Which is really: "WHAT IF I don't go?")

Now turn all of those What Ifs into Won't Its:

- WON'T IT be great when the plane lands safely at my destination?
- WON'T IT be amazing when the plane arrives with its strong wings in tact?
- WON'T IT be great that the pilot did their job well?
- WON'T IT be a relief when I see my suitcase on the luggage carousel?
- WON'T IT be amazing that I am able to keep myself together on the flight?
- WON'T IT be fantastic that I summoned the courage to take this flight?

Hopefully you get the point. If you are a classic "glass half-empty" kind of person, you are just making it worse on yourself. You have nothing to lose by temporarily becoming an optimist (you can always revert back after the flight!). The *language* that you use can very much affect your mindset. Making a "Won't It" statement can instantly change your perspective and the visual images in your head. Again — even if it feels forced or that you're lying to yourself, you must:

1) Recognize your WHAT IFs (whether said aloud or just in your head)
2) Convert them to more positive WON'T ITs.

It might also help to write them down in your book, but I recommend writing down *only* the positive "Won't It" statements – don't bother writing the What Ifs!

3) Courage from Quotes

Don't underestimate the power of quick quotes to help your perspective, whether it's before or during your flight. Write your favorites down in this book, and refer to them as needed. Here are some short, easy to remember quotes on courage that are my personal favorites:

- "Whether you think you can or think you can't — you are right." – Henry Ford
- "The bravest thing you can do when you are not brave is to profess courage and act accordingly." – Corra Harris

- "You must do the thing you think you cannot do." – Eleanor Roosevelt
- "If you wait to do everything until you're sure it's right, you'll probably never do much of anything." – Win Borden
- "The best way out is always through." – Robert Frost
- "Only when we are no longer afraid do we begin to live." – Dorothy Thompson
- "If we're growing, we're always out of our comfort zone." – John Maxwell
- "Courage is simply the willingness to be afraid and act anyway." - Dr. Robert Anthony
- "Courage is not the absence of fear but the judgment that something else is more important than fear." – Meg Cabot

You can also find great quotes on adventure as well as flying; here are a few that I enjoy. Use whatever works for you!

- "I have found adventure in flying, in world travel, in business, and even close at hand... Adventure is a state of mind - and spirit."- Jacqueline Cochran
- "The Wright Brothers created the single greatest cultural force since the invention of writing. The airplane became the first World Wide Web, bringing people, languages, ideas, and values together." - Bill Gates
- "The World is a book, and those who do not travel read only a page. " - St. Augustine

4) See Your Success

Visualization is a common tool you've probably heard of, often used by highly successful people, including top athletes. There are whole books on the topic, but I very simply describe it as envisioning the future you want to see happen. It's not like a written guarantee that it will happen exactly as you wish, but you can get pretty darn close... it tends to depend how much you believe in it and the visions you create for yourself.

Even if you are skeptical about the benefits of visualization and it seems like some floofy thing, I'd ask - what's the harm in trying? All it takes is a few minutes, and it couldn't hurt.

When I use visualization for flying, I focus on how I feel, how I act, respond to the environment – in other words, ***things I have control over*** (me).

It's best to do sit down and try the following visualization exercise at least once or twice before your flight, so that it will be easier to recall and use during your flight if you'd like to.

Sit down (anywhere comfortable) without distractions such as TV, radio, kids, etc. The bathroom is always an option, too, especially if you're in a public place. It's best to close your eyes, but first, read the entire list of things to visualize, and then go through one by one (close your eyes after each statement to visualize it).

Develop the following visualizations (pictures) in your mind in this order:

- Envision yourself the day of your flight, including what you are wearing and how you look - see yourself in a mirror. You are getting ready to go, feeling and appearing relaxed and confident.
- You are leaving on time to go to the airport, allowing plenty of extra time.
- You enjoy a nice drive/ride to the airport.
- As you arrive into the airport area, you look around at all of the planes and moving parts with wonder and amazement. You think to yourself, "Flying is amazing!"
- You are walking into the airport calmly and confidently with your bags. You have plenty of time and feel relaxed.
- You arrive at the ticket check in, wait in line patiently, and you are friendly with the agent.
- You proceed to Security with calmness and ease, with your ID ready to go. You go with the flow through the Security process, being pleasant and helpful to the agents trying to do their jobs.
- After Security, you have plenty of time to stop at the store and buy your water, plus any extra snacks and magazines for the flight.
- You find your gate and it is peaceful, and so are you. You find a chair, sit down and relax.
- You can see your plane, and it looks solid, strong and totally capable of getting you where you need to go.
- You are called to line up, and do so confidently and with ease. You are feeling very patient and not worried about a thing.

- You board the plane, say hi or at least give a smile to the flight attendants, and you feel safe and happy that the flight will begin soon, because it will mean you are closer to your destination.
- The plane taxis and you are so comfortable, with easy access to all of the essentials in your Carry-On bag, which is under the seat in front of you.
- During take-off, you feel a sense of excitement and awe about flight and this incredible journey, going with the flow of the sensations during take-off.
- You are calm and confident through every change in the flight – turns, altitude changes and more. This is a pleasant journey.
- When there is turbulence, you're filled with ease, roll with it and smile a little, knowing that it is only temporary and a very normal thing. You are focused on the task you are doing, or close your eyes and have confidence in finding your courage.
- When the plane starts its final descent, you are excited but calm, knowing that you'll be there soon.
- The plane lands and you are feeling peaceful and proud of yourself for allowing yourself to have a great flight.
- As you exit the plane, you thank the flight crew and proceed to collect your luggage or start your next mode of transportation.

Chapter 17: The Day Before and the Day Of

The critical question at this point is — how are you proceeding with making sure the essentials as listed in Chapter 15 are in your Carry-On bag? Make sure you have **everything** in that checklist, and if not, spend this day making sure you get it all done.

And have you been working on Chapter 16's "Must-Do Mental Preparation?" If not, now is the time to complete all 4 essentials.

If you are the type that is nervous about checking a suitcase in for concern that it will be opened and reviewed or lost, welcome to a new era where, respectfully, you'll need to get over it. Even if you try to cram all your stuff into your Carry-On bags, they don't even allow a lot of the things they used to, and, even if it passes Security's standards, if it's a full flight, it might end up getting checked in anyway. So just be mentally prepared for these possibilities, and make sure the essentials from Chapter 15 are in your **smaller** Carry-On bag.

Most airlines allow online check-in at least 24 hours before the flight time. Even though you will most likely need to wait in line at the airport to check your bag, it's worth the peace of mind to check-in in advance.

While you pack, I want you to think positively about your upcoming flight. Re-read Section 1, plus your Purpose Statement, Courage Quotes and any other concepts that resonate for you, and adopt a good attitude about it, even if it feels forced. Today and tomorrow before the flight, I want you to avoid the TV news and the newspaper.

Think about it this way: how you think about and approach this flight can only be one of two ways: positively (and I count "neutral" as positive in this case) or badly (eg. dread, anger that you have to do it at all, regret). You have two choices on the attitude you have towards this flight, and, it *is* a choice. Why not try positive? "I am looking forward to this trip, and flying is the safest form of transportation in the world…" Even if it feels forced, that's okay; it's better than allowing dread to take over.

Chapter 18: What to Wear

After making sure you have all of the essentials in your smaller Carry-On, what you wear is the next very important consideration. You can either make your flight more stressful by choosing the wrong things to wear, or you mitigate that risk by choosing wisely. There are three principles to remember: 1) ease, 2) warmth, and 3) comfort.

1) Ease: The keywords here are **shoes** and **pockets**. Frequent flyers like me can always spot the rookies — they're the ones with the lace-up shoes, ruffling through their wallets out at the security line to show their ID. Don't add to your own anxiety before your flight – plan ahead in this and sail through various airport obstacles with ease.

Shoes: You almost always have to take off your shoes at the security checkpoint. Thus you should wear shoes that are easy to slip on and off. Avoid shoes with ties and elaborate buckles (eg. sandals) and instead wear slip-ons — and preferably with socks (airplanes get cold!). There are lots of great options nowadays such as hybrid sandal-loafer-sneakers. If you do not want to wear the socks, bring a pair with you in your Carry-On.

Pockets: The following approach will not appeal to everyone, but it's worked well for me for years. I always make sure I have at least two pockets on me, either via my loose-fitting comfy jeans or a front pocket on my shirt. Before I get inside the airport, I put my photo ID in one pocket, and $20 - $40 in another. When I check in at the ticket counter, I just whip out my ID and then put it back in my pocket. Then in the security line, I do the same thing. In some cases you have to show your ID yet again going through the actual metal detector, or at the desk at the airline gate.

The point is that my ID is always handy – no fishing through my wallet or backpack to find it each time. Only when I am finally on the plane do I put my ID back in my wallet. If you think you will forget this step, write a reminder for yourself in this book.

Some might think taking this easy-access pocket approach leaves you more vulnerable to theft. On the contrary, I think it's actually worse to be fishing through your wallet in front of everyone at the airport, and then everyone sees where your wallet goes. I would rather lose or have just my ID stolen rather than my entire wallet.

The accessible cash is so I can quickly buy my bottled water once I get through the security line, plus any magazines that I haven't yet had time to get, and a snack before I get on the plane. All of these things should sound familiar to you as they are listed in your essential Carry-On checklist. And again, use the pocket approach so that you don't waste time fishing in your wallet in front of everyone.

2) Warmth: I don't care if you're coming from 100 degree weather or going to fly into 100 degree weather...***always*** dress in layers, wear pants, and either wear or bring ***socks***. And if you are traveling with kids, the same requirements apply to them.

I always cringe when I see passengers dressed in shorts, short sleeves and flip flops on a flight, only to find that they are freezing once in the air, desperately trying to use those super-thin so-called blankets they provide on the plane (if they're lucky enough to get one).

Don't add to your own agitated state by making the same mistake. No airplane I've ever been on is able to provide a steady temperature throughout the cabin, and even if they could, it might not be to the level to which you are comfortable. It is always colder in certain areas – there are draft zones in certain aisles, and sometimes the window can affect your comfort as well.

You absolutely cannot predict the warmth factor on any flight, even if you're taking off in the middle of summer in Las Vegas! So have a sweatshirt, light jacket or sweater handy at all times, plus your socks, and always wear pants.

3) Comfort: Loose-fitting jeans or sweats are my favorite options. If you are used to wearing tighter pants, that is probably because on the ground you always have the option of being able to change positions (stand up, stretch , lay down, etc.) so your tighter pants don't really bother you so much. On a flight you do not have such options, so being in a sitting position for 2 or more hours wearing tight pants can be a daunting experience. Trust me, I've tried it!

For tops, I recommend a long-sleeved cotton shirt with sleeves easy to roll up, with a thin zip-up sweatshirt. Whatever you choose, remember that the goal is to not add to your anxiety by wearing uncomfortable clothes. You don't need any extra added stress. So dress for ease, warmth, and comfort.

Chapter 19: Arriving at the Airport

As a nervous flyer, arriving at the airport can be the first big trigger of anxiety. It makes the pending flight very real. Here are some effective ways to manage your emotions upon arrival at the airport.

Allow More Time Than You Think You Need

As a nervous flyer, you might not want to spend any more time at the airport than absolutely necessary, but the reason to allow for lots of time is because rushing around and running into longer-than-expected lines will not help your nerves at all. In fact it will make them much worse, even subconsciously.

How early? For domestic flights, I try to get there one hour before I have to board (so 1 ½ hours before the stated departure time). Take the flight time, subtract 30 minutes, and then subtract 60 minutes from there, and that's when I usually arrive.

To make sure I allow for traffic, I take the average time it takes to get to the airport, and then leave 30 minutes earlier.

Even if your flight is running late, get there for the original take-off time anyway. Even if the delay is due to mechanical issues, sometimes they can switch the planes after they announce a delay, then call you to board prior to the latest posted time. I have been "caught" a few times rushing to get back to the gate when a much longer delay was previously announced. Things can change quickly at the airport.

The extra time effort is worth it because it aids in your relaxation. And for a nervous flyer, you want to be as relaxed as possible with the things you *can* control.

Managing Your Feelings

If you are feeling anxious when you first arrive at the airport, I suggest you go straight to check-in, but then before the security line, sit down in a relatively isolated area (or even a bathroom!) to collect your thoughts. Bring out this book and do one or more of the following:

- Review any of the "Ways to Think About Flight" that have resonated best for you.
- Re-read your Purpose Statement on why you are doing this.
- Read to your "Courage Quotes" or other quotes on adventure, flying, or whatever resonates best with you.
- Change your "What Ifs" to "Won't Its (Chapter 16)
- Read the "Making the Numbers Real" (Chapter 6)
- Read a favorite "Pep Talk" (Chapter 43)
- Practice Seeing Your Success (Chapter 16)
- Read any other sections or chapters in this book that help you deal with your feelings.
- If all else fails and you still feel unfocused, count to 25 repeatedly as you continue to go through the motions throughout the airport process. Alter the speed or tone each time you do a round, just to keep your brain busy. Just keep going, knowing you can always change your mind later. No one will force you onto the flight.

Chapter 20: Airport Basics

Steps to Get to the Gate

If you are used to the airport routine, you can probably skip this chapter. But if you fly less than twice a year or if it's your first time, knowing the basics of what to do and in what order can help ease any extra anxieties. Here is a basic overview of each step.

I recommend the following steps in this order: Your airline's ticket counter > Security checkpoint > Gate > Store > Bathroom > Gate

Step #1: Your Airline's Ticket Counter

Nowadays, many airlines let you check in online and print your own boarding pass. This is convenient, but does *not* guarantee that you can skip this step.

You may bypass your airline's ticket counter ONLY if:
- You already have a *printed* boarding pass and NO luggage to check (you have Carry-On luggage only). In that case, please make sure your airline allows more than one Carry-On (some only allow one), that the size of your luggage fits the specifications (you can find this on the carrier's website), and that you don't have any unacceptable materials in your Carry-On.

For all other conditions, you must stop at your airline's ticket counter. For example:

- You already have your printed boarding pass **but** you have to check in luggage
- You've checked in online, but weren't able to print your boarding pass (eg. no/broken printer) (regardless of your luggage situation)
- You do not have your boarding pass (regardless of your luggage situation)

If you're unsure, always go to the ticket counter just in case. It is a real bummer to stand in a long security line only to be told that your 2nd Carry-On is too big and you must go check it in, or, that what you thought was your boarding pass really isn't. Why put your nerves through that test unless you're absolutely sure?

At the ticket counter, always be ready to show your picture ID (a license or passport). Remember the tip on keeping it in an accessible pocket? Here's the first place you have to use it. When done, put it back in your pocket; you'll need it again shortly.

If you want to get your seat changed, the ticket counter is the best place to try. Whatever you do, be courteous. Ticket agents interact with hundreds (if not thousands) of people each day and they can only do so much. Your chances of getting anything changed are higher if you are courteous rather than rude. If they cannot change your seat, be gracious and thank them anyway for trying.

Even if you get through security with two Carry-Ons, don't be surprised if once you're on the plane, you're told that the overhead bins are full and they have to check your larger bag. This happens a lot if you're on a full flight and are in one of the last groups to board. The plane usually does not actually accommodate a full flight's worth of Carry-Ons. This is why it's so important to put all of your essentials into your smaller Carry-On bag that will fit under the seat! (Chapter 15)

Step #2: Security Checkpoint

You need your Gate information to know which Security Checkpoint line to get into. If you got your boarding pass at your airline's ticket counter, it's likely you were told which Gate to go to (or it's written down for you). If you printed your boarding pass at home, all airports have a board that shows which flights are taking off from which Gate numbers.

When you know the Gate number, there are usually signs indicating which Security Checkpoint you should use to get to your Gate. Never assume that any Security Checkpoint will do. You must go **only** to the Security Checkpoint that will get you to your gate. If you don't know, ask someone *before* you get in line.

Be forewarned – in most cases multiple airlines share Security Checkpoints so, don't be surprised if this line is much longer than the line at your airline's ticket counter. However, these lines tend to go faster than it first appears. Everyone who works at the airport is motivated to get you to your flight on time, and they are trying hard to get you through quickly but safely. Unless you do security screening for a living, keep your comments to yourself about the process. Instead, try not to be late to the airport in the first place.

At any point in the Security Checkpoint line – never, ever joke about terrorism, the security process itself, or the security workers. All of these things **will** be taken seriously if overheard and, even if you think you're out of earshot, you might not be, or someone else might feel uncomfortable about your remarks and report you. You have plenty of time in the rest of your life to crack jokes, so trust me – now is not the time (unless you'd like to end up in the security office!).

At some point in the security line (this varies by airport), you will encounter your first screener. All this person does is look at your boarding pass and your ID and make sure your name and image match. They might mark a line on your boarding pass – don't worry about it. Sometimes they will guide you to a specific security station.

Be courteous and go wherever they tell you. Most of the time they just usher you forward into the actual Security Checkpoint itself and you can choose from 2 or more new lines.

As a frequent flyer, it is always painful to watch people be totally unprepared for the actual security screening process, ruffling through their Carry-Ons searching for their documents and having to go through the metal detector several times because they didn't think ahead or pay attention on what they should remove.

Here are some quick tips of what to do, and in what order.

- Have your ID and boarding pass ready (as in: already in your hand) for the first screener, and then keep them very easily accessible for when you walk through the metal detector (again — pockets are great!). In many airports, the person standing at the metal detector will want to see these documents yet again. Don't put them away in a Carry-On and send them through the metal detector; then you'll have to explain it to the metal detector screener, which costs extra time.
- While you are still in the main line waiting, remove your watch, any belts with buckles, hearing aids, large jewelry, and coinage from pockets, and any layers of jackets, sweatshirts or sweaters *ahead of time* and put them into your Carry-On. It is better to just have these things already off and safely tucked in your own bag vs. having to do them all at the last minute.
- When I travel with a laptop or portable media player, I get those out of my Carry-On in advance, and carry them in my hands until I can get them in a tray.

Once you reach the final screening area, the first thing to do is get a few trays out. I recommend you put these things down in this order because it will help you assemble everything faster on the other side:

- Shoes: First, put in your shoes in their own tray (hopefully slip-ons like I recommended)
- Sweater/sweatshirt: In a separate tray put in your jacket/sweatshirt/sweater (if those are not already in your Carry-On)

- Electronics: Put any laptops or portable DVD players (or anything laptop-ish) in their own tray. Usually you can leave your cell phones and audio players in your bag.
- Whole bag: Then put down your Carry-On bag(s)
- Yes, do all of this with your boarding pass and ID either in hand or in your very accessible pocket!

Then wait to be instructed to walk through the metal detector. After you walk through, you will likely have to hand your boarding pass and ID to the agent for yet another quick check.

If through the process they tell you they're going to search and re-screen your bag, don't worry. It's usually a harmless exercise and at least your shoes and jacket will already be back on. Read Chapter 37 for more information about extra security screenings.

Stop #3: Your Gate

Although you might be tempted to stop at a store after Security, always go to your Gate first instead. Even if a status board indicates that your flight is on time or running late, always check at the Gate itself, because that is where the *real* information lives. You will also avoid any undue anxiety if you know where your Gate is ahead of time. If traveling with kid equipment such as a stroller, you must go to the Gate counter and get a special tag.

Stop #4: The Store

You need to bring water on the plane (it's on the Essentials checklist!) – ***do not rely*** upon the flight's food and beverage service. Even if you don't intend to drink it, get it. And since you can't bring your own, you have to get this at an airport store.

Hopefully you already stocked your Carry-On bag with enough snacks and magazines, but, just in case you haven't (or need more), now's your chance.

Yes, the prices can be outrageous, and maybe you never drink water or have an aversion to the concept of all of those plastic bottles. But get the water anyway, even if you also get yourself some juice or soda. Airplanes are dehydrating, and those other drinks will not replenish you like water will if you are delayed on your plane. Get the water and any extra snacks and magazines you need, so that you have less things to worry about.

Stop #5: The Bathroom

Even if you don't feel like you have to go, it's a good idea to go to try now rather than having to do it on the plane before the flight takes off, or while you're in flight having to wait until the captain turns off the seatbelt sign after take-off.

Stop #6: Your Gate - Again

Get back to the Gate as early as you can, and do the following:
- Sit down, even if it means on the floor. It is harder to relax if you are standing.
- Pull out your Purpose Statement and read it; concentrate on it as much as you can.

- Pull out this book and reference any helpful information — hopefully you have earmarked some pages in advance. If not, play a game where you go to random pages and read snippets.
- From Chapter 6: Remind yourself about the numbers. Think about the numbers of people that fly safely every day including the thousands of people accessing this airport today. Notice how peaceful the whole process is considering the volume!
- If you can see your plane, notice how big and strong it is. This might sound odd but, try to befriend the plane in your mind. Say "hi" to your plane, or even give it a name. Doing these things makes the airplane less daunting.

If you have a lot of time:
- People watch and try to guess why they are going the same place you are.
- Call a friend or family member just to chat.
- Do one of the activities suggested in the "In Flight" section.

Chapter 21: Boarding the Plane

Now is the time to think about how you are that much closer to your destination. If you're having a hard time during the boarding process, in addition to the above suggestions, here are a few things to consider:

- Don't pressure yourself; you don't have to board exactly when called. If you need to, take a few minutes to sit back down collect yourself for a few more minutes.
- You can even be the last to board – as long as your smaller Carry-On has what it should, there's no reason to rush yourself!
- See yourself getting off the plane in just a few short hours (however long the flight is scheduled for). You are progressing toward your goal.
- Remind yourself that fight is amazing and that there are thousands of successful flights taking place right this instant, all over the world.
- State to yourself how you feel and allow yourself to feel it. If you're nervous, say to yourself, "I'm nervous." Respect your feelings. Then recognize that it's just that – just a feeling, and thus you have the power to change your feelings at any second. You can decide to feel something else instead, like brave, relaxed, elated, or any other great word that comes to mind. Choose a new word and repeat that a few times instead of the old word.
- Use a perspective statement (from Chapter 11) such as "This is nothing compared to (insert tremendous challenge other people face)."

- Use any other techniques in this book to put yourself at ease, or simply have your magazine in hand
  and flip through it as a distraction.

Each airline approaches the boarding process differently, so just go with the flow. Usually the first groups of
people called to board are first class passengers, people
with special needs, and that airline's frequent flyers. If
you can't hear well (like me), just ask someone next to
you for help; fellow travelers are usually very willing to
help each other.

Once on board, I do **not** recommend that you look
inside the cockpit unless you are truly curious and only
mildly nervous. There is just no need to do it. But if you
can't help yourself and find yourself peering in, I want
you to immediately acknowledge that these people are
total experts at what they're doing and they are just as
comfortable working all of those buttons and controls
as you are in doing your job. Pilots are experts and have
been through extensive training and hours of hands-on
experience relative to what they are expected to do.

Find your seat and if you need help, always ask. But
don't be put off if the flight attendants are not as
friendly and comforting as you wish them to be. Their
primary goal at this phase is to get everyone seated and
situated as **quickly** as possible so that you are not
delayed. They have your time and safety on their mind,
and now is not the time to chit chat with them about
random things. Ask only for help if you need it, or help
others as you see the need.

Once at your row, put your smaller Carry-On underneath the seat in front of you. Don't put it up in the overhead bin, because you need to have it accessible. If you put it above you, you won't be able to access it during take-off, or if there's turbulence and you have to stay seated. Some people think that having a bag under the seat limits your leg room. I have found that the effect is minimal and it's more important to have your bag accessible if your goal is to manage your anxiety.

Next, if you have a larger Carry-On, put that in the overhead bin if room. But be mentally prepared to give it up to the flight attendant. This is why it's so critical to have your Top 10 Essentials in your smaller Carry-On!

Once in your seat, get out this book, your water, a snack or two, and an activity or two (eg. magazine, pen, game, headphones, etc.) into the pocket in front of you. It helps to have a few things accessible before you take off.

When you're settled in, I want you to try to feel grateful. You are about to travel using the safest form of transportation in the world, and save yourself a lot of time and energy. The situation you are in is temporary, and you have a great opportunity to relax and pass the time with a few different things to do. See it simply as that.

Chapter 22: Mechanical Delays

For nervous flyers, hearing the words "mechanical delay" can send the anxiety level up a notch or two. Even worse is when the pilots or the gate crew don't offer any explanation about what the problem is. This can happen while you're still in the airport, or already on the runway.

I believe that airlines are in an awkward situation when informing passengers of mechanical issues, if you think about it from their perspective. Most mechanical issues are minor, because airplanes go through an incredible amount of routine maintenance on a very regular basis. So when there are issues, the airline does not want to cause passengers extra anxiety – both from a flight delay perspective, as well as a safety perspective. They also want to keep you close by the Gate area so that you're ready to go once the problem is fixed, so as not to further delay the flight trying to round up passengers.

I think this is why they don't always go into detail during the broadcast of the delay. In my many flights over the years I have never heard a lengthy description of the reason for a mechanical delay, except when I overhear someone asks for specifics (and then they will usually give more details to that person). But if you don't ask for more detail, the explanation is usually pretty vague.

Also, when a problem first arises, they really do not know how long it will take to fix it. Most people expect the mechanic to appear instantly, but most of the time it takes a while. Once there, the mechanic diagnoses the issue and gives their time estimate. Only then is there a real estimate of the new departure time for the flight.

My point is to be as patient as you can in the process. When I hear "mechanical delay" I instantly equate that to one hour, just to re-set my own expectations. If I'm in the plane, I simply do one of the activities I have prepared for in my Carry-On bag (a great example of why you should have two magazines or games, etc. *per hour* of flight).

If you have concerns about a flight delay and want to know in more detail the reasons why, I encourage you to ask. But if you're a nervous flyer, I must forewarn you that this could be a mistake. Sometimes learning too much information could sabotage your efforts to stay relaxed and calm.

What I tend to do is listen with a curious ear, but not dig for more. This is because I trust the crew and mechanics to know what they're doing.

I think about mechanical delays in a few ways. First, I'm thankful that they found the glitch early, rather than in-flight. That's why they do the tests to begin with! I turn my "What if" into a "Won't it..." As in, "Won't it be great that my flight was safe because they identified an issue before taking off?"

Also, know that airplanes are the most looked over, tested, checked, reviewed pieces of equipment compared to all other forms of public transportation. And consider — for every 100 hours of use, an airplane must go through inspection and routine maintenance, in addition to the standard checks that the pilots do before and during every flight.

If every 100 hours doesn't mean much to you, think of it this way. For cross-country service, most major carriers offer at least 2 departures per day (that's a really low estimate). You might have observed that most of the time when you board a particular plane, it's just been unloaded from the prior flight. Let's say a particular airplane flies back and forth across the country twice a day, for an average 5 hour flight. That's 10 hours a day. So in just 10 days of usage, it's back to inspection and routine maintenance. That's a *lot* of attention to that airplane! Compare to how often you have your car checked (once or twice a year?) yet you use it all the time.

But the next issue is: Let's say there's a spot maintenance issue delaying your flight — do you trust the mechanic to get it right and fix it? I do, and here's why. First, on the many flights I've been on over the past 20 years, I'd say less than 20% of the time there was a delay due to a mechanical issue, either large or small. And all of the flights I've been on have turned out just fine. So first, I always think of the odds.

Next, I've worked with mechanics before. I was a clerk in the mechanic's shop in a food factory for a short stint in college. Although this was a factory they were keeping tuned up (vs. an airplane), it became obvious that you are either born mechanical or not. They always weed out the bad ones – the staff notices it and talks about it – usually because it ends up being a repeat fix. If you're a bad mechanic, it's instantly recognizable... not like if you're a bad business person and can fudge things for a while (no offense intended).

So the odds of a bad mechanic making it through a nearly 2-year licensing program plus oral and practical exams covering a range of 43 technical subjects is incredibly low (to none). And an *un*licensed mechanic cannot work unless supervised by a licensed mechanic, and cannot approve equipment for return to service. I've actually looked up job descriptions for maintenance at a few major airlines, and all require licensing to even be hired (no ad said, "we'll take unlicensed mechanics!"). It might help you to search the internet for "aviation mechanic schools" and read what's required.

Finally, once the issue is fixed, it's thoroughly tested before you take off, and there is collaboration with the pilots and the mechanics. It's not like the mechanic says "Ok I'm done, go on!" It's a team effort to test the fix together.

If at any point you do not feel you have enough information, feel empowered to talk to the gate clerks or ring your flight attendant's call button and simply ask. You are a customer and have a right to know what's going on. They will probably not have much more information than already provided, but, sometimes just hearing it again and that personal attention can make a difference.

SECTION 3: THE PHASES OF FLIGHT

The purpose of this next set of chapters is simply to mentally prepare you for each phases of the flight, including some of the sensations you might feel. I provide basic, common knowledge on how flight actually works – things that I have found easily either on the internet or through my inquiring mind with a few pilot sources. I have for found for myself that a minimum level of knowledge was all that I needed to feel more comfortable – just the basics. If you think you want to know more detail about the mechanics and physics of flight, I would recommend you research a class or book offered by a pilot or airline.

Chapter 23: First Movements

There is usually not some grand announcement once the plane starts moving; instead the flight attendants may start doing their safety announcements and the pilots are doing their final checks while the plane taxis to the runway. This phase has the plane moving rather slowly and uneventfully.

It is important to tune into the flight attendants' safety information. I realize that most nervous flyers don't want to hear lines like "in the event of an emergency," – however, it's important to take note of these things. I think of it not as something to dread, but something to help me be more prepared. Why ***wouldn't*** I want to know where my nearest exits are? What could it hurt to know what the flotation device is? I listen, I get it, then move back to my activity. Do not dwell on this part!

Sometimes the hardest part of the whole flight experience is the anticipation. That's why I look forward to actually getting started... try to view this as a relief... you are now that much closer to reaching your destination successfully!

Chapter 24: On the Runway

The plane will taxi to the runway and usually there is some small wait before taking off; this is due to planes literally lined up waiting to take off. They are not allowed to take off too close to each other, and Air Traffic Control regulates this. The pilots usually communicate with the passengers if there's a delay, and if it will be significant in any way.

At this point, all safety checks are complete and your plane has been deemed safe. A pilot simply does not take off unless the safety checks are complete and good. Safety comes first – there is no pressure for a pilot to fly a plane he/she does not think is air-worthy. They want to make it to their destination just as much as you do.

Delays due to a line-up of other planes waiting to take are usually not significant (over an hour) but it can happen. Again – if you prepared in the way I suggested in Chapter 15, your nerves will not be worse despite the delay.

On the runway is the perfect time to read various sections of this book or a magazine, write, meditate, look at your Courage Quotes, Purpose Statement and anything else that works to keep your nerves under control.

One thing I like to do while waiting on the runway is focus on may favorite Courage Quotes, and then tell myself that I'm excited about taking off. Even if you feel like you're lying to yourself, saying this can make you instantly feel better. I feel grateful that the flight is about to take off, because the sooner we go, the sooner we reach our destination. I anticipate that what we are about to do is totally amazing, and remind myself that this is the safest form of transportation in the world.

Chapter 25: Taking Off

Take -off can be one of the worst times for nervous flyers, but with some re-thinking you can find it exhilarat-
ing and exciting. The process is usually the same each
time; the plane speeds faster and faster on the ground;
the nose of the plane goes up, and the rest follows. It's
loud and rumbly, and you might hear and even feel the
wheels getting tucked into the plane, as well as various
objects shifting in the overhead bins. You might experience sensations in your stomach or head.

I love the thrill of taking off, but I never look around the
plane. I stay focused on the task at hand... usually at
that point, reading a magazine or starting a crossword
puzzle. I sometimes enjoy looking out the window too.
But I don't want to see the parts of the plane itself moving, whether it's the overhead bins or anything else –
even though it's perfectly normal for these things to be
moving. I highly recommend this "heads down"
approach to nervous flyers. You can look around later
after you're cruising smoothly.

Depending on the weather, the land around the airport
(eg. hills or mountains), or other reasons, the climb
feels steeper than other flights. Sometimes take-offs
are it's turbulent, other times smooth. Sometimes you
go straight, sometimes you turn right away. There are
so many variables that influence how the pilot does the
take-off, including Air Traffic Control, weather, sur-
rounding terrain, noise ordinances for that city, time of
day, and more.

How can a big plane with lots of people and luggage on it just simply lift off into the sky? I think about it in a very simple way. Air has mass too, just like water does. You just don't see it. Just like water can feel "strong" to us (eg. waves in the ocean), so can air. When the air is calm, it's effortless to walk through it. When it's really windy, it takes effort; the air feels "strong." Think of it as exponentially super-strong air that is generated by a fast take-off and those powerful engines, and the wings help the plane ride on that strong air.

 Another way to think about is when you're swimming in the water (in this analogy, your body is like an air-plane!). If you are constantly moving (and thus creating moving water), you stay afloat. It's the same principle – the plane keeps moving through the mass that is air.

In a slightly more technical explanation, the wings of planes are slightly curved on top. As the wings move through the air, it divides the air – so that there's air below the wing, and air above of the wing. But because the top of the wing is curved, the air moves faster **over** the wing than it does beneath the wing. So the air pressure above the wing is **less than** the air pressure below the wing. Once the plane goes fast enough (thanks to those powerful engines), this "lift" starts to occur, and the whole plane goes up.

The engines keep the plane going forward during flight and that keeps the lift going. There are at least 2 or more jet engines on every major plane, so even if all but one of those engines pooped out, you would still be fine. But even in the unheard of instance that they all pooped out, the airplane has the ability to glide through the air for miles and miles.

Here are a few things I think about to get my nerves through Take Off:

1) I *yell "Wooo hoooooo"* inside my head. Really! Sometimes it's good to do something totally opposite of what you're thinking to make yourself feel better. If nothing else, it might make you chuckle a little bit. It can't hurt to try!

2) I'm *excited that the process has finally started,* because it means I'm that much closer to reaching my destination, and I marvel at the wonderment of flight – the ability to do this at all.

3) I envision my late Great Aunt Flo as *a giant winged spirit*, swooping in underneath my plane to carry it onward throughout the flight. If you are at all spiritual or believe in guardian angels, this is a comforting vision to have. "Ask" someone who was bold and strong (mentally or physically) in life to be your Flight Guardian Angel. (But if you don't believe in that stuff, keep reading!)

4) At this stage I usually am *flipping through my notes (this book),* including my Purpose State-ment, Courage Quotes, photos, looking a mag-azine or starting an easy crossword.

5) I try to *be relaxed to help others around me who are nervous*. I know I always find comfort when others around me seem so cool-headed,

and it helps you own nerves when you try to help others.

6) I think about the **pilots being totally focused** and relaxed while they do this for the umpteenth time.

7) I **focus my head down and try not to look around the plane too much**. I know that the take-off process causes things to vibrate and move, and it's normal to hear that, just as you do in your car. I just prefer not to **see** it.

8) When I have a window seat, I usually get a streak of courage and **look out at the window** and marvel at the world below.

9) I close my eyes and **meditate,** focusing only on my breath or relaxing each part of my body. (More on meditation in flight in chapter 34).

10) I take **comfort in the numbers** and I also think about the time I was delayed in Denver. I was sitting in the lounge and had a great view, watching plane after plane after plane take off... it was a really peaceful experience. I think about the number of successful flights going on right now (57,500 per day on average).

Chapter 26: Dings, 10,000 Feet and The Slowdown

After take-off, it doesn't take very long to reach 10,000 feet. That is the typical time when you hear a "ding" because it's now safe to use your electronic devices such as audio, video players or video games.

You might hear other dings as well along the way – these can range to a passenger needing assistance, to the pilots or flight attendants wanting to talk with each other, to the need to fasten your seatbelt.

The double-ding of the flight crew wanting to talk to each other always seems to get passengers' attention. If/when you hear this, don't default to negative thinking. The flight crew communicates on a wide range of things – a request for food or drink, a heads-up on turbulence so that they can plan their service times better, information on a potential delay, a sick passenger, and more.

 At some point in your ascent to cruising altitude, the plane might seem to slow down a little. It's a subtle shifting of the speed as well as changes in the engine sounds that you may or may not notice (especially if your headphones are on!).

If you do notice these things, don't worry about it – it might feel odd, but the plane is still moving plenty fast. When I asked a pilot about this, he said quite matter-of-factly that the plane simply may not need to travel as fast as it did for take-off. The speed requirements for continuing to climb or cruising are simply less than the initial take off, and each airport's city noise ordinances also direct how long the plane uses each level of power to take-off. It's also less fuel efficient to keep the same speed as might be required for certain take offs. So do not panic if you happen to feel this sensation.

Sometimes, you will feel a speeding up after you're well into your take-off. Again, this can be considered normal. But the reasons for all of these changes during take-off are dependent on so many variables that it's impossible to give you any consistent patterns regarding take-off — and any attempt to do so would be misleading. Simply try to accept that these variables exist for your safety and in accordance with laws regarding that airport's noise levels, pollution, terrain, and more.

Chapter 27: Turning

Yes, planes have to turn, and often during take-off. I usually handle the minor turns just fine, but the sharper turns can be a little disorienting for the nervous flyer. I handle this situation by doing all I can to get an aisle seat and keeping my head down, simply trying to ignore it. If I have a window seat, I shut the blind or stay very focused on what I'm doing.

But the fact is that turns are very safe, and I trust that the pilots know what they're doing. They could turn a lot steeper than they do – the plane could certainly handle it, but they don't because it would probably freak out a lot of passengers. Consider also that the percentage of time in your overall flight that you are turning is quite small, so I also tend to use the "it's temporary" approach to turns.

How can the planes make such sharp turns and be okay? Think of a bike or motorcycle turning a corner – it leans. Same thing when you fly – the plane leans. Although it might feel like you're leaning a lot or too much – if you could see it from the outside looking in, it's actually not that much at all, and again, it's not even close to the steepness the plane could actually turn safely. Just like turbulence, the pilots are trying to accommodate the passenger's comfort levels, instead of what the plane could actually withstand.

Chapter 28: Cruising

Once you've reached cruising altitude, the pilot should announce this, and, if the air conditions are okay ("smooth air") then you will be allowed to take off your seatbelt and get up to go to the bathroom.

If you were stressed about the take-off at all, this is the time to try to temporarily stop all activities, clear your mind and relax. This is a good time to do this because usually, if you had any turbulence during take-off, it's done now, as the pilots try to find the smoothest air for cruising. They do this not because the plane can't handle turbulence, but because it's more comfortable and safer for everyone in terms of objects on the plane. This doesn't prohibit turbulence later in the flight, but it gives you a nice break.

Depending on the length of the flight, the beginning of cruising is usually when the flight attendants start offering beverages and possibly food. Please have that cash on hand in your accessible pocket as I advised earlier, because it's becoming common place to have to pay for in-flight food (unless you're in first class). Even though you should have plenty of snacks on hand, you might also want what's being served.

It's not uncommon to feel gradual ascents or descents throughout the flight until the final descent. Usually these altitude shifts are usually so minor you'll barely notice them, and often the pilot won't say anything about them. However, if you hit turbulence and the pilot knows it's not going away any time soon, they will often tell you that they're going to try for a different altitude (sometimes up, sometimes down). Do not be alarmed by this...they're doing it for your comfort and physical safety (eg. to not bump your head or spill hot coffee on yourself), **not** because the plane can't handle it. (Keep reading to Chapter 30 for more on turbulence management!)

Throughout the duration of your cruising, which is the majority of the flight, you should be sure to stay hydrated. This means that even if you are drinking other drinks, whether soda, alcohol or juice, you should sip water along the way, too. One approach is to alternate drinks, or even sips. This is important because other drinks are not as hydrating as water (and in fact some are further dehydrating).

The reason why it's so important to make yourself drink water even if you don't want to is because you can become dehydrated faster on an airplane than on land. The more dehydrated you are, the less clearly you think, and if you are nervous, you run the risk of becoming even more agitated. Why make it even harder on yourself?

Some nervous flyers use alcohol to relax, either before or during the flight (or both). Unless you can easily limit yourself with 1 drink before and 1 drink on, I discourage it. First, alcohol is a dehydrator, so that's already working against your nerves. It might feel good and relaxing at first, but once those moments of ease are over, you've just made it harder on yourself. Second, if you depend on alcohol to relax, then you'll just want more and more for the duration of the flight. Then you'll just make it worse for yourself either during descending and landing, or at the airport. Your choice, but, if you do drink alcohol, make yourself drink water with it, alternating sips.

Chapter 29: Sharing the Air

Remember how there are literally thousands of flights occurring in the air all the time? A nervous flyer might wonder why commercial flights never run into each other in the sky.

First, there's Air Traffic Control. Since the dawn of commercial flight, their main job is to put planes in the right places, not just horizontally, but also vertically. There are very strict rules about airspace – the minimum space required between planes and other type of aircraft. There are specific words they must use for various conditions, and pilots must comply (eg. a pilot cannot just take off when *they* think it's clear).

Second, there are collision avoidance systems on most planes nowadays, especially on commercial jets for major airlines. I even have a form of a collision avoidance indicators in my 2006 minivan (beeps when I get too close to something), so I can just imagine what these are like on an airplane! In addition, major airports now have ground tracking radars. The advances in technology like this are tremendous, ongoing, and a source of reassurance.

Third, the pilots within range of each other can talk to each other, and there's also good old-fashioned pilot instinct and "looking where they're going."

Try to think of the last time you heard about two jets from major airliners colliding into each other. You cannot count private planes (even the 2009 tourist crash over the Hudson, which used visual flight rules) because those regulations are not as strict and technology-based as they are for commercial airlines and jets. The incidence of collision nowadays (and even in the past) is unheard of, thanks to all of these checks and balances.

The bottom line is that the pilot has many things at their disposal to maintain their own airspace, from Air Traffic Control, to equipment that just keeps getting better, to their eyeballs. The question is – do you trust them? I do; I believe that pilots have no desire to crash their planes into each other, and that they just want to do their job and do it well, which is to get you (and themselves) from Point A to Point B, safely.

Chapter 30: Turbulence

Many nervous flyers will tell you that the thing that makes them most nervous about flying is turbulence. Turbulence is a phenomenon that can occur at any point in the flight, including take-off and landing.

You often hear that turbulence is like a bumpy road. I tend to think of turbulence more as rough seas. Going back to my "air has mass like water" explanation, think of a boat on rough water. You roll, you go up and down, you can get jolted and tossed around.

In fact, it might help to think about how "boat turbulence" is likely much more dangerous than air turbulence. On a boat, you're usually not wearing a seatbelt, so your risk of injury is greater. You have a false sense of security because you figure if you go overboard, you can simply get back in the boat, but that's not always so in a storm. Also it also takes longer to get out of rough seas; you can't change your altitude to find "smoother waters" like you can in a plane.

So how does the airplane withstand that? Rather easily, actually. Won't the wings fall off? Stop and think about this for a minute. When was the last time you heard of a commercial jet's wing breaking or falling off as the cause of an accident? It might happen as a side-effect of a crash caused by something else, but the thought of a wing just falling off is ridiculous.

Every large commercial jet built is thoroughly tested for extreme turbulence, well beyond what is ever experienced in commercial flight, and the structural integrity of the plane is checked thoroughly with its ongoing inspection and maintenance process.

If you look outside the window at a wing and notice that it is flexing a bit with the changes, that is good. It's designed to flex like that. If it didn't, you'd have a much rougher ride.

The truly dangerous part of turbulence has nothing to do with the plane staying together. Instead it's personal injury, especially if you are not buckled up in your seat. The pilots could probably care less if the whole flight was turbulent; they'd sit there and chat and just get through it, because it's business as usual for them. Trying to get out of turbulence is driven primarily by passenger discomfort and concern for physical safety from moving objects or not being buckled in – eg. spilling drinks on yourself, or hitting something like the ceiling or side wall.

Can pilots predict turbulence? In most cases, they can. Remember how there are literally thousands of flights going on at any given time? There are lots of planes in the sky, and they help each other out, by reporting this "rough air" to Air Traffic Control and to each other. Prior planes give information about the turbulence and how long it might last for the next plane.

Then there are times turbulence can happen just out of the blue; this is exactly why the flight crew encourages you to keep your seat belt on even if the seatbelt sign is off. Personally, I always keep my seatbelt on, albeit a bit looser during easy cruising. So if you suddenly find a turbulent ride but were not forewarned by the pilot, that's normal.

Over the years I've found that there are comforting pilots and less comforting pilots when it comes to talking about turbulence. For a nervous flyer, the friendlier and more comforting the voice of this person in charge of your safety, the better. However, just because a pilot doesn't sound as friendly or comforting, it doesn't mean they're not great at what they do. It's like a doctor with maybe not the best bedside manners.

That said, I really like pilots who talk about it in a comforting, friendly way, such as "well folks, as you can probably tell, we're in some choppy air; Air Traffic (or the plane ahead that just went through it) says it should only be about 10 minutes. So please return to your seats and fasten your seatbelts." When pilots talk like this, it helps you feel like this is all okay and no need to worry.

However, some pilots do a very terse "Fasten your seatbelts" when turbulence hits, and that's it. For the nervous flyer, doing that could make it sound like the pilot's nervous too. It is not the case. First, this is standard fare for them. They go through turbulence every work day, unlike the rest of us. Second, they might be short because they're busy trying to gauge how long it will last (contacting the closest Air Traffic Control or other planes) and then determine if they should stay put or find a new altitude.

I think that in most cases pilots who are really short addressing turbulence just see it as an extra thing they have to do. It's a task and they're getting it done as quickly as possible. It's the same with the initial address... some pilots will talk more and even point out sights along the way or at least tell you where they're at. Some are just trying to get the task off their check-list.

There are a few different ways I like to manage my reaction and nervousness about turbulence. First, I called "Temporary Turbulence." When it starts, I say to myself, "Here's some Temporary Turbulence." It reminds me that this is just a normal part of flight and that it won't be forever. It's simple but effective.

Another favorite and my most used technique is what I call, "Invoke the Spirit of Beth" (my dear adventurous friend). The first year I knew Beth (we met in college), we went on a flight together for a vacation. I was totally petrified of flying, but determined to not let that stop me. I told her how scared I was and she looked at me surprised, and asked why. "Mostly the turbulence," I said. To which she responded, "Oh wow, I *love* turbu-lence! It's so fun, it's like being on a ride in an amuse-ment park. It's a blast, just enjoy it!"

My first reaction was "she's crazy!" But then, on our flight, as we were sitting apart from each other and hit some turbulence, I decided to try her attitude. It was either that or sit there freaking out. Even though it was totally against the way I was feeling, I decided to be fearless and try to enjoy it.

When I did this, I actually found it interesting. I let my resistance go and rode it out. It was a nice relief (and this was a very turbulent flight). Every time my fear started to creep back in, I reminded myself to be like Beth. This is one of many techniques, and it doesn't hurt to try. Sometimes a total change of thinking is what's needed. Even if you can't sustain it for very long, it's an amusing distraction, if nothing else!

Here are other things that help me through turbulence:

1) **Go with the flow,** both physically and mentally. Don't resist the motions. Ride with the changes and don't try to fight it. Close your eyes and talk your body through being relaxed, from the top of your head down.

2) **Know it is only temporary,** as is the whole flight. Trust that the pilots are working hard to get to smoother air.

3) **Know that the plane is just fine** because it's built and tested to extremes, and the main reason the pilots are trying to find smoother air is not because the plane can't handle it, but for our own safety, like spilled drinks or bumped heads.

4) **Think about how a plane going through air turbulence is like a boat going through choppy water,** only safer, because on a boat, you can't just change altitudes to get out of it. Also, I'm buckled in, so it's even safer, thank goodness.

5) **Be grateful for modern airplane technology;** flying used to be a lot more turbulent than it is today. Overall, flying is a much smoother ride than in your car.

6) **Flip through this book** and read snippets or pages your have earmarked.

7) **Picture a massive winged spirit flying underneath the plane;** this can be someone you know who's passed on or just a general vision. Know that he/she is carrying you to your destination safely.

8) **Stay focused on your activity** as best as possible. If it involves anything with writing (like a crossword or a letter), I either find it an interesting challenge to write well during bumpiness, or switch to something easier to do, such as read a magazine.

9) **Try to be a good example** to others who might be nervous by staying calm. Sometimes it is reassuring to others to see someone being totally calm during turbulence.

10) **Close your eyes and imagine** smooth air again, or stepping off the plane at your destination.

Chapter 31: Flying in Clouds

If you bother looking out the window (which I generally discourage for nervous flyers until you start to feel braver), you might notice that occasionally you are flying in a cloud (but most often during take-off and landing). Usually turbulence accompanies that, and you start to wonder — how do they do it? How do we stay right side up? How do we not collide? When will we be out of the cloud?

Because I am usually in an aisle, if I even happen to notice that we are flying through clouds, I try to ignore it and focus on my task at hand. I know that it is only a temporary thing and that it's no big deal to the pilots – this is again something they do every single work day. I also think about the thousands of flights and millions of people flying around the world per day that fly through clouds successfully. The equipment on the plane includes things that indicate how level the plane is, whether it is tilted, and whether or not there is another plane in radar. It's not like the pilots are guessing "oh, yeah, feels like we're ok."

Also, since flying through clouds is most experienced in take-off and landing, both Air Traffic Control and your pilots make sure that the planes are all a very good distance apart. It's not like driving where people can tailgate each other and change lanes any time they want. It's all very strictly controlled – both vertical and horizontal orientation and space apart from each other.

If you're especially nervous during cloud flying, it's important to realize that this is a normal thing for pilots to deal with, and stay focused on things like your Purpose Statement, Courage Quotes, pictures and anything else in this book that resonates for you.

If nothing else, I suggest you simply close your eyes and stop checking to see whether or not the cloud is still there. Looking out the window every minute will only increase your anxiety. Your goal is to decrease the anxiety, so help yourself by closing your eyes and thinking about how brave you are, and Won't It be great when you reach your destination. See yourself at the airport, walking through to the next stop, picking up your bag, getting into your next form of transportation. See how relaxed you are at your destination, whether it's home or a hotel or friend's house.

Chapter 32: Flying in Weather

Even though planes are designed, built, and perfectly capable of flying through rain, snow and storms, pilots and Air Traffic Control will do all they can to go around rough weather. I don't think pilots don't relish the thought of flying through these kinds of conditions any more than you do, but it's more to help your comfort level vs. worrying about the plane being able to withstand it.

To a pilot, flying through weather is par for the course. It's standard. They will go around a storm if at all possible, and there are certain limits on whether or not they will take off during adverse weather, but they are not worried about it the way you might be. The plane is built with redundant systems, and two pilots instead of one (or three, if you want to count auto-pilot!), and does not have the same challenges as say a small private plane might have flying through a storm.

Taking off in rain and standard snow fall doesn't phase me anymore because there are thousands of planes that take off and land in this kind of weather each day. If it's clear that we will be taking off near or around a thunder storm, I remember that I have a choice. If I feel concerned, I'll talk to the gate agent, or I'll try to look up the weather online. If I ever feel too scared to proceed, I won't. (I've never backed out but, it's great to know it is my choice.)

If you find yourself in a situation where you are already on the plane and flying through a storm, try to keep the perspective that in averse weather, you are *much* safer flying in a big plane than driving on the road. And remember that the pilot and Air Traffic Control are working together to keep the plane as far away from it as possible.

It is best to try to keep your focus inward, as I advise for "Flying in Clouds." There is simply an element of trust that you have to give to the plane and the pilots, and the other myriads of people helping to make your flight successful.

Chapter 33: Descending and Landing

The funny thing about descending is that you might not be alerted as to when it's really going to happen. You might think it should happen 30 minutes before the arrival time, but then it doesn't, or maybe it happens sooner than that. Most often the plane will just start to descend —so if you're not focused on the where you are in your flight, it's not always the most comforting thing for a nervous flyer.

I would love to see a rule where pilots have to tell you before they start the descent. But usually you feel the process starting first, and then they'll say something like, "We're starting our descent now."

In my 20 years of frequent flights, however, almost all start to descend 30 – 45 minutes before the arrival time. So if you start to feel the descending at that point, it's not abnormal. And even if you feel it earlier than 45 minutes, it can mean many things – often the pilots can "make up time" and land earlier than scheduled. Or they have been told of turbulent conditions ahead and are proactively going to a different altitude based on the prior plane's experiences.

The reason it varies so much is that the conditions vary so much. Each flight is different. The things affecting the "when" and "how" to descend and land are many, including: the terrain you're landing in (eg. coming in over mountains), the weather and predicted turbu-lence, other planes landing and taking off from the destination airport, the directional orientation of the target runway, etc. Don't even bother trying to predict it!

I am a fan of the long, slow, gradual descents. There are some airports, though, where the landing is quite steep. If you are flying into a location that is particularly close to mountains, for example, you might find yourself in a steep descent (and ascent if flying out).

If this is something you are particularly concerned about, your best bet is to ask the flight crew "what's the descent like into this airport? Is it usually pretty steep?" If anyone can answer the question, it's the people who fly for a living. However, don't be discouraged if they're not sure or say something like, "it depends." It truly does, and they might not know.

When I find myself in a steeper descent than I am comfortable with, I switch gears to inner focus mode. I don't want to look out the window and look around; instead, I close my eyes and go with the flow, knowing it will be over soon.

Personally, I love descending and landing, because it means my journey is almost over and I'm usually excited to get to my destination. I am also proud of myself that I've managed yet another flight, and usually achieved something along the way, whether it was a crossword puzzle or writing an old-fashioned hand-written Thank You note. I take a stance of "I *know* it's going to be okay" and anticipate the bump and rumble of actual landing, which I view as thrilling.

SECTION 4: DISTRACTIONS

In the Top 10 Carry-On Essentials Checklist in chapter 15, I encourage you to bring 2 magazines or easy game per hour of flight, as well as paper and pen/pencil. Those are just the essentials; you can and should also plan on audio, video, hobbies and other distractions depending on the length of your flight.

The bottom line is to be prepared with many potential activities – more than you think you'll need, and the keyword is ***variety***. Again this is to mitigate the impact of flight delays, broken technology, or a boring book. Here are some ideas using what you already have from the Essentials checklist, plus additional things to consider.

Chapter 34: Things to Do

Write to People

Think of someone to write to – your friend, your kid, your spouse, your parent, your politician, your favorite business – just to list a few ideas. Even if you don't regularly think of writing to people, this is one of the best activities for flight.

First, it gets you thinking of someone else and outside of your own head. Second, you always feel better after you do it, because expression of self to others is a basic human need. And since you can't pick up the phone, or text, or go online, then taking the time to write becomes that outlet. The length and format can be a short letter, a long letter, electronic (email) or hand-written – it doesn't matter.

Practical Ideas:

- **Thank You Notes:** Even if you've not had a recent birthday or other occasion to receive gifts, Thank You Notes are a powerful way to feel great and think outside of yourself. Thank someone for: being nice; just being there; being themselves; helping you with some small task; opening up their home to you; making you food; a business that has served you well; your parent for raising you the best they knew how; your kid for just being your kid, the flight crew, etc. There is a never-ending list of reasons to write Thank You Notes if you just stop and think about it for a bit.

- **Write to Yourself:** Write a letter to your future self to open in 1, 5 or 10 years. (Just be sure to stash it in a spot that you'll see it and mark it with an "Open By" date – you will thank yourself later). This is an awesome experience, not just to write it, but to read it later as well. What to say to yourself? Keep it simple so that it doesn't feel like pressure. Write down what you're doing today and basic information about yourself – who's in your life, work information, your hobbies, where you feel you want to change your life, and hopes for the future.
- **Postcards:** Simple and short, postcards are a quick and easy activity to do on a plane. They can be of anything – not just if you've taken some great vacation. You can get postcards of your favorite artists and other paintings and photographs.
- **Your Story:** Write down "the story of your life thus far" to whatever detail you feel comfortable. Note good and bad memories, in some sense of chronology. Write about who you are today and what you're doing. Congrats, you've just started the outline of your autobiography!

Create Lists

These can be practical lists of things you need to do soon, or, a bigger picture "things to do in life" list. Some ideas:

- Things you need or want to do at your destination
- Things you need or want to buy
- Holiday gift ideas for friends and family (or your own wishlist)

- Things you want to get done around the house
- Things you want to make (arts, crafts, woodworking, etc.)
- Movies you want to see
- Books you want to read
- Places you want to travel to in the future
- Classes to take or just things you want to learn how to do
- Goals for money – savings or earnings
- Things you want to get rid of
- Things you want to accomplish in the next 1, 5 and 10 years
- Things you want to tell the people you love
- Ideas for new projects or initiatives for work

Music: Flight & Travel Songs

If you enjoy listening to music on a flight, then in addition to accessing your favorite (upbeat and non-depressing songs), I recommend the following flight & travel songs for download. This is a playlist of positive, classic songs about flying (in some form) that I've used over the years (and makes my age pretty obvious!) Listening to these songs both before and during the flight always helps me feel more courageous and more positively in tune with my flight experience.

Note: This list provides the name of the song and an artist that covers it. It does not necessarily list the author of the song.

- The Three Sunrises – U2
- Learning to Fly – Pink Floyd

- I Can See Clearly Now – Jimmy Cliff
- Fly Away – Lenny Kravitz
- Fly Me to the Moon – Frank Sinatra
- Come Fly With Me – Frank Sinatra
- Jet Airliner – Steve Miller
- I've Been Everywhere – Johnny Cash
- Fly Like an Eagle – Steve Miller

If you are religious or spiritual, I highly recommend songs for your faith on a flight.

Movies or Shows

Movies are an obvious way to keep distracted during flight, and our laptop, DVD players, iPods etc. can be great tools. My advice is to have this only as a secondary option, because you never know when they're going to run out of battery life, or just not work. I also have guidelines for what to watch:

- Stick to comedies or "lite" entertainment. Even if you love action movies, intense dramas or horror films, as a nervous flyer you don't need anything that will raise your anxiety level, and those types of movies do, whether or not you realize it.
- Be appropriate. Nothing makes me madder than when the person sitting next to me puts on an entirely inappropriate movie for an airplane. Whether you like it or not, the person sitting next to you (and that could be a kid!) and likely the people behind you can see your movie, and probably hear it as well. It's easy to say "well just don't look" but it is impossible to just totally ignore intense action scenes and loud noises when the screen is

in such close proximity. And only view movies that are appropriate for a variety of age levels – no greater than PG.

- You have your entire life to watch whatever movies you want to watch in the privacy of your own home. So no excuses on subjecting others to inappropriate content.

Magazines

Magazines are great because nervousness tends to result in a shorter attention span, which is what magazines tend to cater to. Some recommendations – even if you don't normally read these – are things like Reader's Digest, People (a mix of celebrity and human interest stories), and Rolling Stone (even if you are the furthest thing from hip anymore, it always has interesting articles!).

Games

Brain-games like crosswords, Soduku, solitaire and more are a great distraction as well, but again I encourage you to go one level "easier" than you normally do. Although you might think a "good challenge" would be nice and distracting, a flight is not the place for a nervous flyer to add any frustration or tension to the situation.

Electronic handheld games are a great option, but be sure to use headphones (or turn the sound off) so as not to annoy your fellow passengers. Even if you're not the biggest video game fan (like me), there are so many great electronic handheld games today, I believe it is a good investment if you fly even just a few times per year.

Look at Photos

One of my favorite activities on the plane is looking at pictures of family and friends. It's an instant mood lifter!

 In addition to the paper version I ask you to bring in your Carry-On, I normally look at photos on my laptop. There are also so many options for this nowadays including all sizes of digital photo frames that are slim to pack into your Carry-On and can hold a lot of photos.

Be aware that your neighbor will be able to see these as well, so be sure you are comfortable with this, and don't look at anything inappropriate!

Books

If you want to bring a book, just make sure it's not going to bore you. I recommend either one that you've already started that you know you look, a favorite book that you've already read, or something from an author that you consistently like. If you're going to take a chance picking up something totally new at the airport bookstore, don't make it your primary source of activity – be sure to have backup magazines, games, etc. Trust me , there is nothing worse than starting a book on a long flight only to find it totally boring. If it's your only real entertainment option, you begin to feel "stuck," which just makes you more tense and the flight feel longer.

Work or Study

For nervous flyers, doing work or studying for school is a decent distraction on a plane. I have found that I do best with either really "lite" tasks like cleaning out my email or deleting old files, or the other extreme of pondering a big challenge I am trying to solve. Some of my best ideas for work have come from sitting on an airplane and just pondering something from all angles, because you have nothing but time.

The only caution I would give is to make sure you are *in the mood* for work or study – don't force it. It's okay to force yourself to work or study on the ground, but, if you're already a nervous flyer, putting any undue pressure on yourself while on a plane is not wise. Your agitation will increase when you are trying to work or study in a stressful situation such as turbulence or landing.

Whatever you do with work or study, realize that the person(s) sitting next to you can see what you're doing, so be careful with confidential information.

Meditate

Even if you don't normally meditate, meditation is a great thing to try, even if just for a few minutes. It is religion-neutral and is quite simply what I call "exercise for the brain." (An ongoing meditation practice can result in better focus, brainpower, and overall health and peace of mind). It is quite complementary to prayer, and a wonderful way to manage your nervousness in flight.

 The usual recommendation for meditation is to focus on your breathing, but I only recommend that to nervous flyer if you don't think you will worry about your health or hyperventilation on a flight. To do this, simply sit in any comfortable position, close your eyes, and focus your breathing. Don't judge it or try to alter it – no need to try to make your breathing deeper or shallower, or anything else. Just observe what it's like, don't purposely try to change it, and that's it. Keep reading for more tips on how to manage the random thoughts that might come up.

If focusing on breathing sounds too weird, I encourage you to try a body relaxation meditation, where you close your eyes and then focus on relaxing your body from the top-down. Once you finish, you can either repeat it, or mediate on something else, even a key phrase or a visual destination.

Here's a sample body relaxation meditation. Read through the whole way first, then try it:
- Close your eyes
- Put your arms next to you, to the best of your ability, and palms slightly open, facing up or down. On a plane, your goal is to find the most comfortable position that works for you – no crossing of legs needed or other "rules" you might hear about with meditation.

- Focus on the top of your head. Remove all tension, and feel nothing but relaxation on the top of your head. Then say inside yourself, "the top of my head is very calm." (It's easier to say "calm" rather than "relaxed.") Feel the top of your head being calm and relaxed, tension-free.
- Slowly repeat that same thought for: forehead, eyebrows, eyes, ears, mouth, throat, shoulders, chest, upper arms, lower arms, hands, fingers, stomach, thighs, knees, calves, ankles, feet, and toes.
- Don't worry about doing this in perfect order! It's okay to skip around to whatever feels right.

As in all meditation, if/when other thoughts arise during the process, acknowledge them, but then politely send them on their way. It is totally normal to have random thoughts pop up during meditation, and moreso if you're new at it, so don't get discouraged, no matter what frequency they come up. Envision yourself as a mountain, and any distracting thoughts are simply clouds passing by. Don't get upset about them or let them bother you. It takes many years of mediation to be able to maintain solid focus, and all you're doing is practicing, so don't put any pressure on yourself.

If you're analytical and start questioning the mountain analogy because mountains actually have a lot of activity going on within them, simply think of it like your human body. As still as you are able to sit, there is always a ton of activity going on within your body – blood pumping, cells moving, etc. Don't overthink it!

How will you feel afterwards? There is no pressure to feel *any* particular way after you meditate, but the ideal is that you will feel relaxed and calm, and perhaps even a pleasant "buzz." If you feel frustrated because you think you did it "wrong" then I strongly encourage you to stop putting such pressure on yourself! Look at it as "just another thing to do" and consider trying it again. The key is to not pressure yourself into thinking you need some great result – that is the opposite goal of meditation.

If it does make you feel better, even just a little bit, it has served its purpose. I encourage you consider meditation in your daily life because it's such a great brain exercise (it's religion-neutral and has the potential to enrich your life).

Other suggestions for meditative focus, in addition to body relaxation:
- A favorite scene in nature
- Light and warmth radiating throughout your body
- Numbers (counting to 100 and back, for example)
- A favorite phrase or series of phrases

Take a Break

This might sound odd but, sometimes a trip to the bathroom is a great distraction. It helps to just to stand up, stretch your legs, take a brief walk, check yourself out in the mirror and splash some water on your face (or as I prefer, bring facial wipes). If you are sitting in the recommended aisle seat, doing this a few times during your flight is fairly easy.

Be sure not to be a bathroom hog, though, and always wait until the seatbelt sign is not fastened. If you are waiting in line and the seatbelt sign comes on, you should get back to your seat (unless it's a bathroom emergency!).

Another way to take a break is just to go stand at the back of the plane. If you do this, be prepared to hang out with the bathroom crowd, or have a flight attendant ask what you need. They might need the space – so make it brief.

If you are not seated in First Class, most airlines do not allow you to use the First Class bathroom. It may seem ridiculous, but, this is typical. If you are in First Class, do not wait up at the front for the bathroom – it's not allowed anymore.

Other Hobbies

If you have other hobbies that are non-invasive to others (eg. can be done in a small space and don't smell or are distracting) then I encourage you to bring them along. For example, knitting/crocheting needles are allowed, but scissors are generally not (nothing with a razor-type quality to it). Gluing model parts probably comes with an invasive smell. Markers and crayons are acceptable for artwork, but probably not paints.

You can always check tsa.gov online to get a list of prohibited items if you're not sure. If you don't see the items you're interested in listed, you can email or call them.

SECTION 5: SPECIAL ISSUES

There are a variety of "special issues" that can come up during flight, most of which you have very little control over. What you **do** have control over is how you let these things affect you, and in some cases, how you react or respond. Here are some of these issues, with suggestions on how to keep perspective and manage the situation.

Chapter 35: Babies and Kids – Not Your Own

I used to dread sitting near babies and kids on flights. I was already nervous enough; I didn't want the additional stress of listening to crying babies, upset kids, and — even worse — upset parents who didn't bring enough activities for their restless child.

I'd like to say my thinking changed when I had my own kids, but it really hasn't. I still don't enjoy sitting near other's kids (even though I love kids) because I have seen too many times where the **parents** are not proactive in anticipating their kid's needs, and frankly, it bothers me. However, it is often unavoidable. There isn't a "family section" on planes, and you could very well be in an unpleasant situation for the duration of your flight.

The most important thing I want you to consider if you are sitting near upset little ones is that it's **not the baby's or kid's fault**. They don't have the ability to control their emotions as we grown-ups do; when we get upset, scared, or angry, we know how to keep it inside (for the most part). Kids don't – their emotions are pretty much outward until their brains are further developed. So if you become agitated, don't focus it on the child. And if an older child is unruly, it is because they have been allowed to be unruly, or, in some cases they have developmental issues that make them act out.

Most parents try their best to contain their kids while on a flight, but I have seen plenty of times where parents actually get angry at their kids, which almost always makes it worse. Not only do you have an upset kid, but an upset adult in close proximity.

Some approaches for the nervous flyer are:
- Discretely ask the flight attendant to move to another seat on the plane, if it's not full.
- Try to help the parent by either offering to help them get things from bags (not easy to do in a cramped space), or engaging the child with peek-a-boo. Peek-a-boo almost always works wonders, if even just for a few minutes.
- If you see a parent get angry at their kids and the situation is getting worse, you can say something like, "It's hard enough for me to sit in one spot for 3 hours – I can't imagine how much harder it is for a child that age! Is there something I can do to help?" This can help both the parent and the kid.
- You might even consider carrying a small set of crayons and paper in your bag... or a finger puppet... these small things can work wonders for almost all ages.

- Babies cry due to changes in their ears among many other reasons... there might be nothing the parent or you can do, so make sure you have your noise-reducing headphones – it's in the Top 10 Essentials for your smaller Carry-On bag!
- Take frequent breaks – in this case, a break is a trip to the bathroom – to collect yourself.
- Remember that babies and kids have just as much right to be on that airplane as you do. The situation you're in is temporary, and the more you let it affect you, the more nervous you are going to become. Try to have empathy for the children – they don't want to be in this situation either!

Chapter 36: Babies and Kids – Your Own

For nervous flyers, the challenge with babies and kids is even greater than for people who have no concerns about flying. You have to manage not only your kids, but the myriad of feelings you experience for yourself about flight. You must step up as best you can to be the strong and courageous parent you would want for yourself. Empower yourself – do all you can to prepare well both for yourself and your kids' sakes before the flight, using this book and focusing on this chapter.

Once I had children of my own, flights changed from being a time to relax, read magazines and be introspective into **work**. You owe it to your kids as well as your fellow passengers to do all you can to keep your child relaxed, occupied, well-hydrated, well-fed and safe on the plane. If you're going to fly with kids, you must treat it as one of the more difficult tasks you are going to have as a parent, and approach it like a project, with great preparation.

Nothing bothers me more than seeing parents totally baffled and angry at their kids during a flight. They act as though the coloring book and crayons and one toy they brought along should be enough to keep their little one happy. They feel embarrassed and use anger to try to shush their kids.

Kids are unable to be mentally prepared for an airplane ride like adults are. They have more energy, they have a natural need to explore, and they don't like being confined to one spot under any condition. They don't know how to control their emotions the way we do; they are outward whereas we know better to try to keep our emotions inside as appropriate.

Thus airplanes and kids are just a bad mixture. Albeit a necessary one – kids have just as much right to be on that plane as anyone else. But, it's a tough combination, and you must go in thinking not so much about your needs, but moreso for your kids' needs.

A kid on a plane who is unruly or upset on a flight is not to blame. If you as a parent are not armed with multiple activities and with a mindset of this flight being work and ***not your time***, then you are to blame. And I'm speaking as a stepmom and mom – having flown multiple times with my family ranging from brand new baby to 10 year old.

The only exception are babies – if you have done all you can to make sure they are not hungry and are trying your best to entertain, they still might cry due to ear pressure or just wanting a change of scenery.

All that's asked is that you do your best. I could proba-bly write a whole book on this subject alone, but here are my strong recommendations for managing kids on an airplane, so that your nerves and your fellow pas-senger's nerves stay calm.

- Mentally prepare your kid (even if 1 – 2 years old) at least 1 day before the flight in a very enthusias-tic tone that you are going to be going on a plane ride and that it's going to be very fun, you are going to bring lots of fun things to do, and that you expect them to behave well (not in a threatening way, but in a matter-of-fact way). Then ***repeat*** – a lot – throughout the hours before the flight, in the car on the way to the airport, then once you get inside the airport, and then again at the gate... you get the idea. Preparing them, setting expectations and reinforcing this is critical.

- If any of your kids are below age 5, request to sit at the back of the plane, or if flying an open seating carrier, seat yourself in the back. I'm sure some parents would protest this and say that they should feel free to sit anywhere. But it is my strong opinion that families with young kids should be towards the back. Why? Because unless you are flying first class, you will be 1) closest to the Emergency Exits, 2) closest to the bathrooms, and 3) it is courteous to the frequent flyers that tend to be towards the front of the plane.
- If it's just you and one child, I recommend that you choose a middle-window seat combination.
- Try your best to board early – most airlines offer this option.
- If your kid is 2 or older, they must have their own seat, and thus get a Carry-On allotment too, so you should have no problems packing everything you need as your smaller Carry-Ons. I recommend checking all other luggage other than those smaller Carry-Ons that can fit under the seat.
- Avoid the bulkhead seats (no seat in front of you) because you will have to put all Carry-Ons above you, and seat pockets are smaller, if present at all. I once thought it would be great to have the extra leg room, but it turned into a fiasco.

- The minimum amount of distractions (toys, books, games etc.) you should pack in your Carry-Ons is **4 per hour of flight** for any child over the age of 6 months. So if you are taking a 5 hour flight, this means 20 distractions. I'm not joking. This might sound like a lot, but it's just the minimum, as I'm sure you've noticed that the attention span of your child is significantly smaller than us adults.
- Choose distractions wisely so that they will fit into your bags, along with the other essentials I've listed. You don't have to use the original packaging; you can use baggies to hold Play-doh or puzzle pieces instead, for example.
- Your job is to keep 2 – 4 distractions plus snacks in the seat pocket in front of you at all times, and to rotate quickly as needed. The rest should be available in your Carry-On under the seat in front of you.
- Here are recommended distractions that can be small and easy to pack, listed from younger to older, but always choose age-appropriate toys!
- Teething ring
- Small stuffed animals
- Rattle or similar
- Plastic rings that connect/disconnect
- Mirror (babies love to look at themselves!)
- Picture books
- Small photo album with pictures of family and friends
- Finger puppets
- Any other kind of puppets
- Lego blocks (age-appropriate size) – small baggie's worth

- Stickers
- Plastic animals
- Play-doh – just 1 – 2 colors and 1 – 2 gadgets (but nothing knife-like!) in a baggie
- Story books
- Small magnetic doodle board
- Coloring books
- Blank paper including a few sheets of construction paper
- Washable crayons or markers
- Self-contained stamps (no ink pad needed and test that the result is washable)
- Water-based coloring books (dip brush in water only and color appears)
- Foam picture frames
- Glue stick and foam appliqués – eg. for the frames and/or to make birthday cards for others
- Flashcards with pictures with words
- Toy cars (eg. HotWheels or Matchbox) or toy airplanes
- Games like Uno or matching games
- Puzzles with larger pieces (that you wouldn't mind losing and don't want to keep assembled)
- Slide viewers (eg. View Master)
- Kids' camera
- DVD player w/ DVDs and headphones (be sure they are willing to wear headphones, or watch without sound)
- Electronic hand-held games – age appropriate, (eg. Leapfrog brand, or Nintendo for older kids)
- Word search and other games book and pencil
- Book about airplanes

- Travel Diary and pen (if not writing yet, you write what they say)
- Bring 2 snacks per every hour of flight, and make sure it is a good variety of options. Now is not the time to be strict about a food schedule; snacks are a great distraction as well.
- Recommended snacks that are easy to pack (as always, be sure they are age-appropriate):
- Rice puff snacks (for babies; there are a few good brands out there)
- Fruit bars (soft to chew)
- Crackers (graham crackers are a good choice)
- Animal or alphabet cookies or any other shapes that you can talk about
- Goldfish (they come in baby-sized too, now)
- Cheerios
- Easy-peel (Clementine) oranges
- Bananas
- Apple slices (easy to find pre-sliced in small bags, even at fast food chains now)
- String cheese
- Fruit roll-ups
- Water!
- Age appropriate cups; don't use what flight attendants hand out until kids are older, eg. 4 or 5
- Bring lots of clean-wipes, even up to age 5.
- ***Never*** leave your child under age 5 unattended in a seat while you use the bathroom! Not only could it be scary for them, but even though you're on a plane, it's totally unsafe. If they're small enough, take them into the bathroom with you. If age 4 – 5, take them with you and ask the flight attendant if they can stand nearby them until you are done.

- I do not recommend taking children under 4 for a "walk on the plane" because when you return to your seats, they will just feel more restricted — thus the odds of having a fit go up. Instead, let them stretch by standing up in their seat and looking around. If you have to go to the bathroom, I recommend that you carry them the whole way so that the idea of getting to walk around is not even introduced.
- For children age 4 and up, getting up for a walk is a good idea. But before you go, explain that the walk is just for a minute and that you will be returning to your seats shortly.
- Although most airlines allow children under 2 to sit on your lap instead of their own seat, I think it's crazy to try this after 6 months of age. It sounds tempting to save the money, but, in addition to being unsafe in my opinion, your sanity is in for a big test, and it's worse if you're a nervous flyer. Not only does it greatly restrict your room, but it gives far less movement options for the child. It is simply more humane to provide their own seat, and you will be relieved as well. However, for babies that do have their own seat, a car seat is required up until the age of 2. If you are willing to buy a child under 2 their own ticket, usually you can get a discounted fare.
- There is an FAA-approved alternative to a car seat for your under-2 year old. I've used it and it works quite well; go to kidsflysafe.com.
- Getting angry at your kids on an airplane is totally inappropriate not just for your kid, but also for your fellow passengers, and will ultimately back-

fire on you. Although they can't articulate it – taking a flight is not a fun experience for them (after the novelty has faded). A crowded airplane is not the time and place for discipline; it's the time and place to distract, entertain, and appease. Considering that the majority of your time is on the ground, don't make it unpleasant for your fellow passengers and give your kids a break. It's ok to feel frustration, but make sure it doesn't turn into anger.

- For babies: Try your best to time feeding so that it is during take-off and landing. This will help minimize ear pressure.
- Not wanting to pass your nervousness on to your kids can be very motivating for the nervous flyer.

Chapter 37: Extra Security Screening

If you end up at the "special" screening station alto-gether, it means they're going to do extra screening on you, usually involving a search of your Carry-On bags and use a metal detector wand to scan your body.

If this happens to you, do not question them on why – I've had this happen a number of times and although it is really annoying, most of the time it's a random selec-tion process. I don't know the politics of whether peo-ple of select ethnicities get pulled for this special screening more than others, although I've certainly heard that opinion.

Although it can be nerve-wracking to get this extra screening, it is just something you need to do to get through. You may be asked to remove jewelry, and then all layers such as a jacket or outer layer sweatshirt or sweater, and your belt and shoes and perhaps socks. All of those are fair game for removal. However, you should never be asked to remove anything beyond that.

Try to keep in mind (as they are wanding you) that these workers are average people trying to do their job, which is to determine if random people are carrying explosives or other weapons on the plane. The inten-tion is good even if the process for us average folks just trying to get on the plane is not pleasant. Whether or not you agree with the concept is beside the point.

If you still feel you are pulled unjustly for this screening or violated during the process, you have the right to write down what happened and the names of the people that worked on the process, and follow up as you wish. You can also ask to talk with a supervisor – but if you do this again, please be courteous. The goal is to get to your flight.

Chapter 38: Old Planes

I'll never forget the day I stepped on to a plane only to find an ashtray in the armrest (and this was on a major, very successful airline). Smoking has not been allowed on flights in many years, and I was taken aback wondering, "how old is this thing?! Can this possibly be safe?"

Before that flight took off, I had to convince myself that all would be fine. I flipped through my book and the thought that helped me most was — do you really think that not just 1, but 2 pilots would jeopardize their lives by flying in an airplane they felt was too old and unworthy?

The flight ended up perfectly fine, as usual, but I did some research online afterwards. I already knew the FAA had strict safety standards, but learned that those become even stricter as the plane gets older. The number of years a commercial passenger plane can stay in service seems to vary, taking into consideration several factors, such as its age, flight miles, and number of take offs and landings. You could find yourself in a 20+ year-old plane on any given airline. That sounds like a long time, but in reality, the airplane is constantly maintained and parts and structure are replaced as needed over the years, even modernized flying systems and instruments, and its "skin" as needed.

So while it might seem like an old jet, it's actually a constantly reviewed, maintained and updated jet. (Wouldn't it be nice if we could replace parts of our body in the same way?)

And frankly, if I were running an airline business and thus interested in managing costs, I too would replace all of the mechanical and structural parts first before I replaced the more cosmetic parts, like armrests!

I don't even try to figure out how old a plane is; I trust the limits and standards in place. And I believe that the pilots in charge of inspecting the plane before take-off and getting us to our destination want to complete a successful flight as much as I do, so I trust their judgment.

Chapter 39: Over Water

Clearly the planes we fly in are very capable of traveling vast distances without needing to stop or refuel – otherwise there wouldn't be thousands of overseas flights every single day to all reaches of the earth. And although it feels like you might be "all alone out there" you are not; nowadays your plane is almost always in connection with an Air Traffic Controller center or other planes heading towards the same or nearby destinations.

Just for fun, I did a very simple search for a non-stop round trip flight from LA to land in Sydney, Australia on a particular day (a trip I've successfully made a number of times). Seven major airlines popped up with different departure and arrival times. Two of them looked like the same flight (airline partners) so let's say there were only 5 non-stops from LAX to Sydney. Then I checked to make sure those flights were offered every day.

The result is that there at least 5 non-stops per day to Sydney from LA, plus one from San Francisco, plus one from Vancouver, BC. So there are at least 7 flights per day from the West Coast just going to Sydney, plus the same amount flying back the other direction – that's 14 a day making one of the longest over-water routes. That translates into over 5000 flights per year across the Pacific Ocean, just to one destination. Add to that the daily flights going over-water to get to Sydney from Japan, Hong Kong, Singapore, Europe, Africa, New Zealand, and more. (To get to Australia from anywhere, you pretty much have to fly over a good stretch of water!)

When is the last time you heard about a major commercial flight to or from Sydney having issues? Ever? And let's say the absolute worst did happen – a water landing **can** be successful as a plane is built to glide, and obviously the manufacturers think so as they put flotation devices including life jackets in every seat. And since the flights are so tracked nowadays, help would likely arrive within a reasonable period of time.

All that said — you should even waste your time thinking that way! Instead, I want you to enjoy your overwater flight because the odds are so greatly for your success, and if you're going over any significant body of water from the US, you are likely going someplace wonderful and with a great spirit of adventure – a new country, or an exotic locale. Keep your destination in mind.

Chapter 40: Chatterers

People on flights have different mindsets – some like to talk, and others want to be totally introverted. As one who enjoys the solitude, I have found that most people either leave you alone or make small talk, and then it drops. But if you happen to end up near a chatterer, it can add to your stress level, and for some it can be awkward to end the conversation.

If you **want** to talk with someone, great, because it could help pass the time and possibly make you more relaxed!

But if the chit chat is making you annoyed or more nervous, you have a few options. Choose what you're most comfortable with and works best for your personality.

Give hints:
- Pull out your noise-reducing headphones and have them in your hand.
- Have your magazine or other activity in your hands and up; keep glancing at it while you're responding.
- Close your eyes while responding.
- If possible, excuse yourself and go to the bathroom; when you come back, just dive into an activity without saying anything.
- If at any time you feel you are being harassed in any way, get up and talk to the flight attendant, or, if the seatbelt sign is on, write a quick note that you need help, ring the flight attendant button and hand it to them. (Or if it's really bad, just be blunt about it!)

Use a Transition Statement:
- "Well, I promised myself I would get some work done so I need to get started – but it's been nice talking with you!"
- "It's been nice talking but I promised myself I would use this time to re-charge and relax so – I'm going to escape into my head for a while now!"
- "Hey – maybe we can talk again later, like during the descent? I promised myself I would conquer this puzzle and focus on a few other things during this flight."
- "I wish I could chat more, but I'm a nervous flyer and I feel calmer when I focus on the activities I have planned."

If **you** are the chatterer, be considerate and look for clues that people want to end the conversation and focus on their own things. Better yet, simply say, "Well you probably want some time to yourself, but if you want to chat some more just let me know." If the person truly wants to keep talking, they'll continue the conversation. If not, they'll be grateful for your consideration and take advantage of your offer.

Chapter 41: Managing Panic Attacks and Extreme Stress

I've had only one panic attack in my life and although it wasn't on a plane, it was definitely one of the most unpleasant experiences I've ever had. I was 6 months pregnant at the time, at work, but not doing anything particularly stressful; it seemed like nothing really triggered it, yet suddenly I could not control my emotions and felt like I couldn't breathe.

A panic attack can be followed by certain triggers, or in my case, seemingly out of the blue. For a nervous flyer, a plane ride could trigger a panic attack, even if all is going well. Or it could be a more specific trigger, like flying through a storm, or over water, or feeling trapped.

If at any time you feel yourself heading in the direction of a panic attack, there are a number of things you can try to do (read on for suggestions), but *if they're not working*, you owe it to yourself and your neighbors to ring the flight attendant button. Explain that you think you are having a panic attack and need some help to get over it. The flight crew can assist you with oxygen if needed and will try to calm you down. You can ask (or might be asked) to move to another part of the plane, if there's room.

The key thing is *don't be embarrassed*. Nowadays people know enough about panic attacks as a phenomenon that can happen to anyone. The flight crew has a vested interest in helping you, because they don't want others to start panicking either (and also because most have compassion and want to help people).

If it makes you feel better, you can try to do what I did when I had mine – I kept apologizing to everyone in between sobs saying, "it's *just* a panic attack" because I didn't want people to think it was something worse, and I was still able to provide this level of objectivity. However, you don't have to nor need to justify this medical issue.

If you feel panic coming on, there are some things you can to try to head it off before it escalates. I'm convinced that the only reason I've not had a panic attack on a flight for all of these years is that I have used these techniques. However, it's not a guarantee, and as I've mentioned, panic attacks are much more understood nowadays. If you reach a point where you feel you need help, you should get it.

Recommendations for Managing Feelings of Panic

Please note – I am not a medical expert, and the following is simply advice of things that have worked for me. If you have concerns about how to manage a panic attack, or experience recurring panic attacks, please see your doctor prior to your flight.

1) Research Panic Attack management ahead of time: Researching how to handle panic attacks before the flight should help you feel more empowered and prepared, which in turn will help you manage your emotions during the flight.
- Research online (try a reputable medical site such as webmd.com) or talk to your doctor about how to manage a panic attack, including hyperventilation.

- If your doctor advises anti-anxiety medication, be sure to **try it** at least twice **before** you fly. A flight is **definitely not** a time to try out a new medication. Anti-anxiety medication can be very helpful, but the point is to test it before you're on the plane.
- If you have concerns about a medical condition and whether or not it is advised to fly, talk to your doctor. Don't add more stress to your flight by worrying about whether or not it's safe for you to be there in the first place.

2) Focus on the right things: Once you have the information you need, do not worry about feelings of panic or anxiety. Worrying about whether or not you will have a panic attack might actually increase your odds of having one. Decide to keep an empowered attitude that you are filled with courage and are going to get through this flight just fine. Focus on how flight is amazing, that it's a temporary situation you chose to optimize your time, and that you will be successful.

3) Try coping techniques: If you start to feel like you're losing it, flip through this book to help you remember more coping techniques. But the main point is to not pressure yourself to stick with any one thing. If something's not working (even if it helped you before), go on to the next thing; there is no need to feel disappointed if it doesn't work. Different things work at different times.

4) Let go a little: You might reach a point where you just feel agitated "trying things." At this point, let go. Put down any activities, close your eyes and let the plane carry you along. Simply repeat something positive to yourself, such as "I am courageous," or "This is much safer than driving" or "All is good." Let yourself become part of the flight. I have found in my worst moments that doing this for a while resets my brain. It is okay to go through many feelings, phases and levels of patience throughout a flight.

5) Ring the flight attendant: As I referred to earlier, if you reach a point where you need help, don't be shy about asking for it. Getting help when you need it benefits not only you but also your fellow passengers.

As politely as possible, tell the flight attendant that you need help calming down and would appreciate anything they could do or say to help. They might try to talk you through it right there, or have you move to another section (if it's possible or safe to do so), find a doctor or nurse on the plane, or simply suggest a magazine and check in with you once in a while.

They want to keep everyone calm, so they'll do what they can, but recognize that they are not doctors. The worst thing to do is to get frustrated with them if you feel they are not helping enough; it will just escalate your anxiety as well as theirs. Be very clear about what you need – it's much different to say "I'm having a panic attack" vs. "I'm having a panic attack and I need your help – anything you can do would be appreciated."

Chapter 42: Claustrophobia

For some people, a feeling of claustrophobia or being trapped is large part of what makes them nervous flyers. This can be in addition to actual nervousness about the flight process itself.

I can very much relate to claustrophobia when it comes to small spaces, which for me is more like an elevator rather than a plane. I actually find the inside of a plane to be plenty of room, and unlike being trapped in an elevator, I know approximately when I'll be able to leave!

Many of the ideas in this book might help the claustrophobic flyer, such as keeping a clear Purpose Statement, putting fear into perspective (the "This is nothing compared to..." statements), Courage Quotes, distractions, meditation, and so forth. Here are some additional thoughts:

- Claustrophobia in and of itself is a legitimate phobia that can be treated with the help of a professional psychologist or program, and if you have any issues in this regard, I highly encourage that you seek treatment for this. If you are claustrophobic on a plane, then it's likely that there are other scenarios (elevators, other small spaces) where seeking professional treatment or at least investing in a few good books could help.
- Don't fly anything smaller than a 737. Before you book your reservation, always check. Most online booking sites that I've used list the type of airplane.

- For long flights, consider what would work best for you: The first approach is to break up long cross-country or international flights into a few flights so that you have the opportunity to get a break. Make sure the breaks are significant or even over-nighters – not the usual 1 hour layovers. If you go this route, I recommend working with a travel agent. The second approach is to take the most direct trip with the least amount of stops in an effort to just get it over with. When weighing these approaches, consider what it is that makes you the most nervous about flight, and what feels most manageable. Go with your gut on this.
- Always get an aisle seat – which means book well in advance.
- Prepare for the flight mentally by envisioning success; see yourself getting through the flight feeling very relaxed.
- Consider using anti-anxiety medication (as discussed in the prior chapter). Discuss the options with your doctor, and be sure to test how you react to any medication prior to the flight.
- Remind yourself that this is simply a temporary situation and that it will be over with soon. This journey is with purpose, and you have not found yourself "stuck" in an unexpected situation.
- Tell yourself repeatedly that the airplane is "more than enough room."
- Get up and walk around during cruising periods so that you feel less restricted to your seat.
- Plan for and bring many distractions to keep your mind away from obsessive thinking.
- Feel empowered to ask the flight crew for help should you need it.

Chapter 43: Pep Talks

As your "Portable Flight Coach" I would be remiss if I didn't give you a pep talk when you needed it most. Pretend I am sitting in the seat next to you as the ultimate example of calmness and strength, saying these reassuring things to you.

I actually try to be this way on flights because I know there are a lot of nervous flyers out there, and when I was a nervous flyer, it was of great help if I had a neighbor who seemed perfectly calm and relaxed during turbulence, for example.

Here are a few different pep talks to choose from.

Slightly Nervous

Hi! How are you feeling? If you're feeling a little nervous, that's okay – don't put pressure on yourself to feel anything but what you feel. But know that I'm proud of you – you did it, you got on this plane and you're on your way to your destination.

You're doing great. You are one of millions of airplane travelers just today alone, and there is a whole giant workforce that flies for a living, all the time. You are in a solid plane that is constantly kept tuned-up, and in the hands of not just one but two expert pilots who love what they do. You'll be at your destination before you know it, and you have saved yourself lots of time by traveling this way – the safest form of transportation in the world.

You are courageous and bold! Keep going, you're doing great.

Very Nervous

Hi! If you're scared, I'm here to help. I remember how it felt to be really nervous on a flight, and I'm here to tell you that what you're going through is just temporary. You are stronger than you know, and you're doing fine. What is your Purpose Statement – why are you here? Dig into that well of courage I know you have within you.

I want you to *not* look around; instead stay focused on yourself in this book. I can relate, and I'm here to tell you that I've been on over a thousand flights that have turned out just fine. You can do this.

Remember that despite any misgivings you may have at this moment, you are traveling in the safest form of transportation in the world. You have nothing to fear, and you can get through this. You should be proud of yourself already.

What is your favorite Courage Quote? Think of it and repeat it now. Let yourself feel like the brave adventurer that you are. You will soon be back on the ground – just picture yourself walking off the plane with a big smile on your face.

Now I want you to either continue with visualizing reaching your destination or doing something you enjoy; or do the relaxation meditation, or read a new magazine. Drink some water, keep your head down on your activity, and stay focused in your own little world until you feel calmer. You have the strength to do this, trust me!

Flight is Amazing

Hi! Isn't this flight amazing? It is such a thrill to fly – from the fast take-off, to cruising, to landing – it's an awesome experience, especially if you can ease your tension and let your body and mind just go with the flow.

So many people have worked to make your flight experience a great one – from the folks who designed, built, and tested this airplane extensively, to the airport's ground crew, the ticket clerks, the security guards, the gate attendants, Air Traffic Control crews, the flight attendants and the pilots. Here you are, able to fly through the air in this incredible machine – it is ingenious.

The pioneers of flight would be blown away today with the advances of airplanes over the years, many of which were designed to make your flight a more comfortable one – less turbulence, many more safety features, more options for entertainment, and the ability to fly for longer periods so that you have less stops to make. Enjoy this flight by allowing yourself to focus on the great things about it. Flight is amazing!

Spiritual – God

What if God created birds and other winged creatures to inspire us to fly, and then He gave us the knowledge and ability to figure it out? The invention and advancement of flight has saved millions of people throughout the world – by providing the transfer of food, medicine, and people wanting to help others – bringing so many people together. Like all things, we can choose to look at the blessings provided and focus on those.

Let us pray right now, not just for ourselves and our safety, but also in thankfulness for the pilots and flight attendants helping us in our journey; let us also be grateful for the blessings this flight brings to us, whether it's to see family, friends, vacation or our work.

Let us be thankful for the opportunity to have such an experience – to be up in the heavens close to God, and to see the earth below from His perspective. Appreciate the beauty of His creations in the sky and the universe — the sun, the moons, the clouds, the stars. Surely He gave us this gift to help us slow down a little and bring us perspective.

SECTION 6: POST-FLIGHT

Chapter 44: Looking Forward

Congratulations – you did it! You have successfully arrived at your destination. I hope that any of the concepts in this book helped you get through your flight in a more relaxed way (or daresay, even enjoy parts of it!). You should take pride in your achievement.

Even if the last thing you want to do is spend any more time thinking about flying, take a few minutes now to help yourself in the future (especially if you have a return flight coming up). The fresher these things are in your memory, the better they will help you next time.

First, make some notes in the back of this book on how you felt during the flight. What were the parts that were you felt the most relaxed? The most stressed?

Next, earmark or highlight any techniques in this book that worked for you – whether it was any new or different ways to think about flight, the statistics, or any other ideas or techniques. And if you can, write your own as well.

Third, think about your Carry-On – did you have enough things, and/or the right kind of things? What would you change for next time (except lowering the quantity...again, always assume your flight will be delayed, even if this one wasn't). Note what you want to do differently next time.

Fourth, put this book away in a spot you will easily remember for your next flight, perhaps even your standard Carry-On bag or suitcase.

Finally, write to me via **nervousflyer.com** and let me know how it went. I'm always interested in success stories, as well as how I can improve as a "Flight Coach" for the future.

Happy Flying!

REFERENCES

1 - Barbara Rothbaum, psychiatry professor and head of the Trauma and Anxiety Recovery Program of the Emory University School of Medicine in Atlanta
2 – Statistical Summary of Commercial Jet Airplane Accidents, Worldwide Operations 1959 – 2008, reported by Boeing (statistics include other brands of jets, not just Boeing)
3 – US Department of Transportation website
4 – Airline Pilots Assocation website

YOUR NOTES

YOUR NOTES

YOUR NOTES

YOUR NOTES

YOUR NOTES

YOUR NOTES

YOUR NOTES

YOUR NOTES

YOUR NOTES

YOUR NOTES

YOUR NOTES

YOUR NOTES

CPSIA information can be obtained at www.ICGtesting.com
Printed in the USA
LVOW070839141112

307252LV00007B/10/P